# Professional Studies in the Primary School

*Also available:*

*Foundations of Primary Teaching* (3rd edition) (1–84312–131-X)
Denis Hayes

*Professional Values and Practice: Meeting the Standards* (3rd edition) (1–84312–384–3)
Edited by Mike Cole

*Unlocking Creativity: Teaching across the Curriculum* (1-84312-092-5)
Edited by Robert Fisher and Mary Williams

# Professional Studies in the Primary School

## Thinking Beyond the Standards

Eve English and Lynn Newton

David Fulton Publishers

David Fulton Publishers Ltd
The Chiswick Centre, 414 Chiswick High Road, London W4 5TF

www.fultonpublishers.co.uk

David Fulton Publishers is a division of Granada Learning Limited, part of ITV plc.

*British Library Cataloguing in Publication Data*
A catalogue record for this book is available from the British Library.

ISBN: 1 84312 206 5

10 9 8 7 6 5 4 3 2 1

Typeset by RefineCatch Ltd, Bungay, Suffolk
Printed and bound in Great Britain

# Contents

# About the contributors

**Helen Cardy** is a deputy head teacher and a partnership school training centre co-ordinator. She contributes to the Core Issues module on aspects of assessment for the PGCE primary trainees.

**Eve English** is Course Leader for the Primary PGCE programme and Lecturer in English at the University of Durham. Her research interests include interactive teaching, mentoring on teacher training programmes and issues related to partnership. Her publications include *Meeting the Standards in . . . Primary English* (RoutledgeFalmer 2005).

**Tracey Hume** is a primary teacher and a specialist in Special Educational Needs.

**Linda Johnston** is a primary head teacher who works with Durham University on various aspects of its generic skills programme, particularly in the area of PSHE. She mentors trainees in her school.

**Teresa Leggett** is a deputy head teacher and partnership training centre co-ordinator. She contributes to the Core Issues module on aspects of behaviour management for the PGCE primary trainees.

**Douglas P. Newton** is a specialist in science education and also in the psychology of education. His particular interest is in teaching for understanding and he has written many books and articles on various aspects of education, including *Teaching for Understanding* (RoutledgeFalmer 2001). He is Professor of Education at the University of Newcastle upon Tyne and also Professorial Fellow in Education at the University of Durham.

**Lynn Newton** is Director of Initial Teacher Training and Professor of Primary Education at the University of Durham. Her interests include primary science and design technology and she has written widely on these subjects, including *Meeting the Standards in . . . Primary Science* (RoutledgeFalmer 2000).

**Catherine Worton** is a primary head teacher who contributes to the primary initial teacher training undergraduate course on aspects of early years education. She mentors trainees in her school.

# Preface

Initial teacher training is the first step in a career as a teacher. Teaching is, without doubt, a challenging profession; as a process, it never stands still. As learners, the children you teach will be constantly changing and challenging the teachers who work with them to be imaginative and motivating. Therefore, you, as a teacher, cannot stand still either. You need to be constantly balancing maintaining the *status quo* with moving forward and developing in your role. During your training it is likely that you will be required to meet a number of government standards for initial teacher training to demonstrate your readiness to take responsibility for a class. Your training programme, whether undergraduate or postgraduate, will be designed with this in mind; it will encourage a fusion of theoretical perspectives with practical experience. This book is designed to help you to think about issues more broadly than a narrow focus on standards might allow. The aim of the book is to encourage you to be a thoughtful, and hence effective, practitioner.

Each chapter is written by an expert who has a particular interest in the area being discussed, and concludes with some suggestions for further reading to take you more deeply into those issues. In bringing together each expert's thoughts, the chapters are slightly different in style and organisation, reflecting their diverse contents, but all contain common elements which include:

- a theoretical perspective on the relevant issues;
- practical applications and strategies;
- illuminative case studies to exemplify thinking and practice;
- suggested activities for you to try; and
- recommended further reading.

In Chapter 1, *Teachers as professionals: the background*, Eve English considers recent developments and initiatives in terms of the curriculum and organisation of schools. An understanding of these issues will help you reflect on your own teaching and make decisions about the effectiveness of new initiatives.

In Chapter 2, *The reflective practitioner*, Lynn Newton discusses the origins of the concept of reflective practice and the implications for trainees as teachers in the twenty-first century. The relationships between teaching and learning and the complexity of the planning and assessment cycle are considered.

In Chapter 3, *Teachers and the law*, Lynn Newton looks at the professional and legal requirements that any teacher must satisfy. Your duty of care and your statutory responsibilities as a teacher are highlighted. Untangling the complexity of the legal framework in which we work is not easy but pointers are given for you to think about.

In Chapter 4, *Teaching and learning in the primary school*, Doug Newton provides a succinct overview of issues underpinning effective teaching and learning, including what makes an expert teacher effective. The role of motivation and relevance is emphasised and related to the process of planning for teaching and learning.

In Chapter 5, *Planning for teaching and learning*, Eve English considers all aspects of effective planning, including the importance of the planning/assessment cycle, which leads into the discussion in Chapter 6 on assessment.

In Chapter 6, *Monitoring and assessing learning*, Helen Cardy discusses what we mean by assessment and the important differences between the various types, purposes and methods of assessment.

In Chapter 7, *Behaviour management*, Teresa Leggett begins with a nightmare scenario. Fortunately, this is only a dream and she takes you through well-used strategies to ensure that the nightmare does not turn into reality for you.

In Chapter 8, *Classroom approaches and organisation*, Catherine Worton takes you through the competing pedagogies that you will encounter in your role as primary teacher and advises you on the selection of appropriate learning experiences for pupils.

In Chapter 9, *The individual in the primary classroom*, Lynn Newton looks at issues underpinning the needs of all pupils in terms of providing equal opportunities, regardless of age, ability, gender or cultural background. The concept of differentiation is introduced and discussed.

In Chapter 10, *Different needs and different responses*, Tracey Hume builds on the issues introduced in Chapter 9 and develops them for particular groups of children with special educational needs. She also includes reference to the needs of gifted and talented pupils.

In Chapter 11, *Personal, Social and Health Education and Citizenship*, Linda Johnston explores ideas behind this whole issue. She emphasises how PSHE&C can provide children with the life-enriching experiences that may not be found elsewhere in the curriculum.

In the final chapter, *The way ahead*, Eve English guides you through the process of applying for jobs and being interviewed. She explores issues related to the induction year and offers case studies on the role of the curriculum leader/co-ordinator.

Going beyond the UK government's standards, this book will be valuable for you as a novice or newly qualified teacher, wherever you teach.

Eve English and Lynn Newton
University of Durham
March 2005

# Teachers as professionals: the background

## Eve English

## Introduction

Welcome to the first stage of your teaching career. You will be very well aware that you have chosen a profession that seems to be subject to constant change and is forever in the media spotlight. It is certainly a challenging career, demanding your time and energy, but, at the same time, very rewarding. You have the opportunity to make a difference to children's lives; and you only have to think back to the important teachers in your own school education to realise that good teachers are not forgotten.

So where do you fit in? This first chapter will place you as a trainee teacher in the current educational climate. It will consider recent developments and initiatives in terms of the curriculum and organisation of schools. It is important that you have an understanding of what has led up to the curriculum that you will be required to teach. This understanding will help you reflect on your own teaching and make decisions about the effectiveness of new initiatives. Changes have not only taken place in schools, of course; the actual training of teachers has also been subject to upheaval, and this will also be discussed.

## Primary education – recent developments

The 1988 Education Reform Act brought about far-reaching changes in education. The advent of the National Curriculum and the monitoring and assessment of that Curriculum was part of the Act. When you, as a trainee teacher, go in to schools, first as an observer and later as a fully fledged teacher, you will be prepared for and familiar with the requirements and the structure of the Curriculum, but for teachers in 1988 the Curriculum (both content and delivery) was changed in a way that they could never have imagined. Up to this point teachers had decided what they were going to teach and how they were going to teach it. The content of the curriculum and the style in which it was delivered differed from school to school, and often from class to class. It was not uncommon for Mrs A. to be teaching a child-centred curriculum in one classroom – attempting to address the needs of all the individual pupils but doing little direct teaching – while next door Mr B. was delivering very formal, undifferentiated lessons where all teaching consisted of whole-class lessons. Very often head teachers would not intervene in the teaching process and formal planning and assessment were minimal. While teachers were influenced by research, courses and advice from the local education authorities, in the end the responsibility for the teaching of pupils in a particular class belonged to the teacher. This all changed very dramatically with the introduction of the National Curriculum. The 'what to teach' was determined by the National Curriculum; and the 'how to teach' was later prescribed by the National Literacy Strategy (NLS) (DfEE 1998a) and the National Numeracy Strategy (NNS) (DfEE 1998b).

What led to these changes? Concerns about standards in education and accountability were, and continue to be, the major factors underpinning the changes. You will be very aware that the media, as well as employers, educationists and taxpayers, have an interest in standards. Every year, in August, the newspapers are full of headlines about the supposed decline in A-level standards. This concern begins much earlier in the education process with the publication in newspapers of Key Stage 2 Standard Assessment Task (SATs) results, comparing the results of different schools and LEAs.

Throughout the 1970s there was much debate surrounding standards and accountability and this came to a head with the Labour Prime Minister James Callaghan's speech to Ruskin College Oxford in 1976 when he spoke of 'core curriculum subjects', 'national standards' and 'the role of the inspectorate'. The 'Great Debate' followed Callaghan's speech, resulting in the publication of the Green Paper (DES 1977). This focused on a need for a national core curriculum and also for schools to become more accountable. The 1988 Education Reform Act pulled together the intense debate that took place throughout the 1980s, following the Ruskin speech and the Green Paper, and the National Curriculum was born. The National Curriculum was introduced gradually from 1989 and was revised in 1995 and again in 2000. The NLS was implemented in 1998 and the NNS in 1999. These two strategies are not statutory but are strongly recommended.

You need to make yourself familiar with the structure and content of the National Curriculum. But first let us think of the main aims of education. Before we look at the educational aims as set out in the National Curriculum, try the first activity.

## Activity 1.1

What would you consider to be the main aims of education in the twenty-first century?

How do your aims compare with those stated in the most recent National Curriculum (DfEE/QCA 1999) orders?:

Aim 1: The school curriculum should aim to provide opportunities for all pupils to learn and to achieve.

Aim 2: The school curriculum should aim to promote pupils' spiritual, moral, social and cultural development and prepare all pupils for the opportunities, responsibilities and experiences of life.

(DfEE and QCA 1999: 11)

Within those broad aims there are requirements that schools should encourage pupils' progress through a stimulating curriculum that equips them with the 'essential learning skills of literacy, numeracy, and information and communication technology, and promote an enquiring mind and capacity to think rationally' (*ibid.*: 11). The two aims reflect section 351 of the Education Act 1996 which requires that:

all maintained schools provide a balanced and broadly based curriculum that:

- promotes the spiritual, moral, cultural, mental and physical development of pupils at the school and of society;
- prepares pupils at the school for the opportunities, responsibilities and experiences of adult life.

(*ibid.*: 12)

The four main purposes of the National Curriculum are:

- to establish entitlement for all pupils
- to establish standards
- to promote continuity and coherence; and
- to promote public understanding.

## Activity 1.2

Think about the purposes described above and consider how, before the National Curriculum, there might have been problems in ensuring that all pupils had an appropriate curriculum.

The 'broad and balanced' nature of the curriculum has been questioned of late and new documentation is seeking to address concerns (see below). But, first of all, it is important that you find your way around the National Curriculum.

## Structure and organisation of the National Curriculum

The National Curriculum divides schooling into key stages. In primary schools, Key Stage 1 relates to Years 1 and 2 while Key Stage 2 consists of Years 3 to 6. The Reception year is now part of the Foundation Stage, which has its own curriculum – *Curriculum Guidance for the Foundation Stage* (QCA/DfEE 2000) – and covers ages 3 to 5.

For Key Stages 1 and 2 there are ten subjects. Three of these are core subjects (English, Maths and Science) and seven are foundation subjects (Design & Technology, Information & Communication Technology, History, Geography, Art & Design, Music, and Physical Education). In Wales, where the language of instruction in schools is Welsh, Welsh itself is also a core subject. In addition, all schools are required to teach Religious Education according to a locally agreed curriculum. For each core and foundation subject, and for each key stage, there are programmes of study. These set out the content, skills and processes that pupils should be taught. Attainment targets (ATs) set out the 'knowledge, skills and understanding that pupils of different abilities and maturities are expected to have by the end of each key stage' (DfEE and QCA 1999, Attainment Targets: 1). To sum up, the programmes of study set out what is to be taught while the attainment targets assess that learning. ATs consist of level descriptors of increasing difficulty and teachers use these to describe their pupils' performance. At Key Stage 1 the majority of pupils are expected to work within levels 1 to 3 while at Key Stage 2 the levels are 2 to 5. The same levels are used in the Standard Assessment Tasks that pupils take at the end of the key stages.

## Activity 1.3

(This activity is designed to help you find your way around the National Curriculum.)
*Observe a lesson in school. Is the lesson a core or foundation subject?*
*Discuss with the teacher the learning objective of the lesson.*
*Find, in the subject's programme of study, the content to which the learning objective relates.*

## The National Literacy Strategy

The National Literacy Strategy (NLS) was introduced into schools in September 1998. The Strategy followed a pilot Literacy Project that involved 18 local education authorities during the years 1997 and 1998. While the NLS is not statutory, it is highly recommended, and it was initially expected that the approach and content of the NLS would be adopted by all primary schools unless they could demonstrate that end-of-key-stage SAT results demonstrated that existing arrangements were at least as effective. There is more flexibility now, but in September 1998 schools were expected to provide a dedicated, continuous hour of literacy teaching each day in all classes. The NLS Framework for teaching (DfEE 1998a) gives very clear directions on how the Literacy Hour is to be divided up into whole-class shared reading and writing, guided and independent work and a plenary session. The content, as well as the structure, of the NLS is very prescriptive. The teaching objectives are set out year by year and, from Year 1 onwards, term by term. The introduction to the Framework describes a 'searchlight' approach (DfEE 1998a: 3) to the teaching of literacy based on an interactionist approach (see Stanovich and Stanovich 1995) where successful readers are seen as those who use as many strategies as possible, including knowledge of phonics, word recognition, grammar and context.

If class teachers' autonomy was threatened by the National Curriculum then the even more prescriptive National Literacy Strategy was quite alarming to many. Beard (1999) produced a rationale that considered the theoretical underpinning to the NLS, but many educational researchers were as critical of the strategy as were classroom teachers. The fact that speaking and listening were hardly addressed was a major criticism as was the reduced level of interaction between teacher and pupil that resulted as teachers produced 'pacey' lessons to meet the required objectives (English *et al.* 2003). Cajkler (1999) was also very critical of the misconceptions contained in the NLS. The title of his paper ('Misconceptions in the NLS: National Literacy Strategy or No Linguistic Sense?') says it all.

The NLS has addressed the lack of speaking and listening skills by producing new documentation, *Speaking, Listening and Learning: Working with Children in Key Stages 1 and 2* (DfES/QCA 2003), and the National Primary Strategy (DfES 2003, see below 'Excellence and enjoyment: a strategy for primary schools') is encouraging schools to take ownership of the curriculum and be more creative. Many schools, as a result, are moving away from the rigid structure of the NLS.

## Activity 1.4

Look at page 9 of the NLS Framework (DfEE 1998a) which sets out the structure of the NLS. Compare this structure with the way in which you have seen literacy teaching organised in schools.

## The National Numeracy Strategy

The National Numeracy Strategy (NNS) was launched in 1998 and formally implemented in schools in September 1999. As with the NLS it is very prescriptive and there is a framework that sets out teaching objectives for each year of primary schooling from Reception to Year 6. Many skills have been introduced at an earlier age than was previously the case. A typical daily numeracy lesson uses a three-part structure, starting with oral work and mental calculation using whole-class teaching. The main part of the lesson is used for teaching new topics or consolidating previous work. The final plenary session involves the whole class and allows the teacher to draw together what has been learned. Again, as was the case with the introduction of the NLS, a national training programme was set up and run at a local level by newly appointed co-ordinators using videos showing good practice. It has been claimed by the government that the NNS has been an undisputed success. This has been questioned by researchers (e.g. Brown *et al.* 2003).

# Curriculum guidance for the Foundation Stage

September 2000 saw the introduction of a Foundation Stage for children aged 3 to the end of Reception year. To support this Foundation Stage, the QCA (Qualifications and Curriculum Authority) has developed accompanying curriculum guidance *Curriculum Guidance for the Foundation Stage* (QCA/DfEE 2000). For the first time in this country, pre-school and Reception year children have been provided with their own curriculum that purports to be relevant to their needs. For teachers of pre-school children a common curriculum is provided regardless of the educational setting. For teachers of Reception year children there is now a recognition that all children in that year group need a discrete curriculum, and it removes the previous confusion that arose from the requirement that a child should follow the National Curriculum from his/her fifth birthday. The Foundation curriculum is designed to help early years practitioners plan towards the Early Learning Goals (QCA 1999). These replaced the *Desirable Outcomes for Children's Learning* (SCAA 1996). These Early Learning Goals describe expectations deemed to be achievable for most children by the end of the Foundation Stage. In this way they are equivalent to the attainment targets of the National Curriculum.

There has been some concern (e.g. Edwards and Knight 1994) that the curriculum offered to young children has been a diluted version of the National Curriculum and that teachers have been finding it difficult 'to sustain the well-established principles of early childhood education in their practice' (Early Years Curriculum Group 1998).

The *Curriculum Guidance for the Foundation Stage* (QCA/DfEE 2000) is providing the opportunity for practitioners to build on their knowledge of child development and to provide a curriculum that is more appropriate to the needs of young children. The guidance is divided into four sections; the two main sections address, first of all, the principles and supporting practice for effective early years education and then the areas of learning and Early Learning Goals (p. 11).

Having outlined the principles for effective practice in early years settings, the document provides supporting descriptions of what these principles mean and practical examples of how they can be turned into good practice. In this same section (QCA/DfEE 2000: 20–4) effective learning and teaching are described and clearly explained.

> Learning for young children is a rewarding and enjoyable experience in which they explore, investigate, discover, create, practise, rehearse, repeat, revise and consolidate their developing knowledge, skills, understanding and attitudes. During the foundation stage, many of these aspects of learning are brought together effectively through playing and talking. (*ibid.*: 20)

> Teaching means systematically helping children to learn so that they are helped to make connections in their learning and are actively led forward, as well as helped to reflect on what they have already learned. (*ibid.*: 22)

Again, this section gives clear practical examples of how the theory can be translated into good practice, each example easily recognised by early years practitioners as a way in which children can be assisted in their understanding.

The other main section addresses the areas of learning and early learning goals. The guidance is providing a curriculum that supports the attainment of Early Learning Goals (QCA/DfEE 1999). These goals are organised into six areas of learning that are almost identical to the earlier *Desirable Outcomes for Children's Learning* (SCAA 1996). The areas are: personal, social and emotional development; communication, language and literacy; mathematical development; knowledge and understanding of the world; physical development; and creative development. The supporting curriculum guidance is quick to point out that the areas are defined in order to assist practitioners with the planning of experiences and activities and not to suggest that children's understanding can be divided into discrete areas.

The guidance takes each area and identifies 'stepping stones' of progress towards the Early Learning Goals. The knowledge, skills, understanding and attitudes that children will need to achieve the goals are described. The stepping stones are supported by practical examples of what children may typically do at the various stages and what the practitioner needs to do. Again, the QCA makes quite explicit the fact that although the stepping stones are presented in a hierarchical order it should not be expected that all children will conform to the sequence.

The value of play and active learning is very much acknowledged by the QCA/DfEE's (2000) guidance. Mathematical understanding, for example, is seen as being developed through stories, songs, games and imaginative play (p. 68) and, again, the practitioner is given many examples of practical activities to help the children on their way to attaining the Early Learning Goals.

## Excellence and enjoyment: a strategy for primary schools

The latest addition to the requirements for schools in implementing a curriculum is the document entitled 'Excellence and enjoyment: a strategy for primary schools' (DfES 2003). This attempts to address the concerns of all those who feel that creative aspects of the curriculum and foundation subjects have been marginalised by the teaching of core subjects as schools strive to reach end-of-key-stage targets. It also addresses the complaints of teachers that their professional judgement has not been sufficiently recognised:

> A central message of this document [*Excellence and Enjoyment*] is that teachers have the power to decide how they teach, and that the Government supports that. (DfES 2003: 16)

The document addresses other issues, but in terms of the curriculum it is giving teachers permission to be innovative and develop the character of their individual schools.

The case study that follows describes one school's response to *Excellence and Enjoyment*. It illustrates the belief that standards do not need to decline, and can indeed be enhanced by a curriculum that seeks to motivate pupils through the 'fusion of excellence and enjoyment' (Clarke 2003).

## Case study 1.1

The new primary strategy came just at the right time for one junior school with 214 pupils in the north of England. The school is in what Ofsted describes as a 'mixed catchment area with high levels of deprivation in some parts'. This phrase describes an ex-mining village with high levels of unemployment but where new housing is attracting more 'upwardly mobile' families. Before the introduction of the primary strategy the staff had already decided that the curriculum, based on the NLS and NNS in particular, was not suiting their pupils and they were concerned that SAT results had 'plateaued'. They were particularly concerned about what they saw as the fragmented nature of the NLS. They have, therefore, chosen to concentrate more on the text-level aspects of the NLS, particularly the need for children to read, and have read to them, whole books rather than the 'snippets' that they had been using to illustrate particular objectives. Drama and Speaking and Listening have returned to the school's curriculum in an attempt to introduce more creativity. A half-term English topic will now involve the study of one text or non-fiction topic and all word-, sentence- and text-level objectives will be met through the enjoyment of that text.

The school always prided itself on its broad and balanced curriculum and felt that the foundation subjects had never been marginalised. However, they are now looking at more cross-curricular links (where the links are meaningful and appropriate) and 'blocking' subjects, so that history, for example, is taught in a more concentrated way rather than being spread over the whole year.

The members of staff feel that a more creative curriculum will motivate their children and, in doing so, will increase levels of attainment.

## Teacher training – recent developments

The concerns about standards and accountability that resulted in a national curriculum for schools have also been at the centre of changes in teacher training. In 1997 a government circular (DfEE 1997) introduced a national curriculum for Initial Teacher Training (ITT) that sought to ensure that all trainee teachers received training that the government thought was appropriate and would prepare them for the schools in which they would be working. The original criteria included a list of standards that all trainees should meet to be awarded Qualified Teacher Status (QTS), the Initial Teacher Training curricula for English and maths and the requirements of all ITT institutions. The list of standards related to the subject knowledge of the trainee, the ability of the trainee to apply the skills, knowledge and understanding of teaching and learning in the classroom, and criteria related to the planning, management and assessment of learning and behaviour. As in schools, Ofsted began to inspect teacher training institutions to ensure that all criteria were being met.

In 1998 a new circular (Circular 4/98) entitled *Teaching: High Status, High Standards* was issued. This extended the criteria for Initial Teacher Training. As well as generic Standards for the award of QTS the new document specified ITT national curricula for English, Maths and Science and a national curriculum for the use of Information and Communication Technology (ICT) in subject teaching.

As well as changes in terms of central control of the ITT curriculum there has been a shift in the partnerships between higher education institutions (HEIs) and schools. We have moved from a model in which schools provided 'teaching practice' places for trainees, but had minimal responsibility, to one in which schools and HEIs are seen as partners. This new model is the result of Circulars 3/84, 24/89, 9/92 and 14/93 which specify that schools should take on increased responsibility for the training of teachers rather than their earlier more supervisory role. Circular 9/92 talks about partner schools and expects those schools to have at least joint responsibility for the planning and management of courses. The responsibility was delineated in that HEIs were to be responsible for course accreditation, procedure, certification and placement of trainees in schools. Schools were to be responsible for classroom base competence. The latest standards and requirements that replace DfEE Circular 4/98 (DfES Circular 02/02, 2002) have a focus on generic elements of training, although the subject knowledge is still an expectation.

Certainly, these changes cannot be separated from the political climate. Wilkin (1994) describes the ideology that supports the greater responsibility of schools in the training of teachers and the diminishing role of HEIs. She says that what the government wants is a teacher who has skills but is not 'critically reflective about the process of education and the teacher's role as a practitioner within it' (p. 9). Edwards (1995) similarly describes a 'highly politicised restructuring of initial teacher education' (p. 8). Wilkin and Edwards were describing the political climate under a Conservative government, but there has been no indication that a Labour government is in any hurry to reverse the trend and move back to a situation where schools once again take a marginal role in the training of teachers. This is not to say that HEIs have been hostile to the new arrangements. From the 1970s, ITT institutions and schools had already been moving towards a form of partnership where schools were being encouraged to take on more responsibility. Newton (1995: 70) describes how few tutors from HEIs are likely to oppose the principle of partnership so long as both sides of the partnership recognise the expertise of the other. The following case study describes the partnership between one ITT institution and its partnership schools.

## Case study 1.2

One university in the north of England has changed its partnership arrangements with its partner schools on both the BA (Ed) and PGCE courses so that the schools have even more responsibility than they had in the past. The partnership involves the university, school training centres (STCs) (with a co-ordinator (STCC) in each of these centres), and complementary cluster schools (CCSs). The STCCs play a crucial role in the new arrangements, taking over responsibilities that were usually held by university tutors, even in recent years. The STCCs meet the trainees who are going to be in their clusters right at the beginning of the course, during the induction period. They organise much of the practical training of the trainees and they place the trainees in appropriate schools within their clusters. Class teachers and link tutors (mentors) in individual schools assess the trainees against the standards but the STCCs support the schools and moderate the assessment of the trainees in their cluster schools. University tutors have a quality assurance role in moderating assessment across all the clusters. The university still ensures that the trainees' subject knowledge meets the required standards, but much of the application of that knowledge is organised and assessed by the schools.

The trainees have a home area school experience before they actually join the course. The workbook of activities associated with this placement is assessed by the STCCs. The trainees then have meetings at the beginning of the course with the STCC in which prior school experiences are reviewed and priorities are set for the future. Within the clusters the trainees visit a variety of schools to observe good teaching practice. This takes place during weekly visits of one day a week and blocks of weeks. The STCCs ensure that their trainees have experience of different key stages (including Foundation and Key Stage 3) and of children with a range of abilities and needs. The STCCs also contribute to lectures on generic professional issues. Seminars are held throughout the year in STCs, and STCCs advise on planning; monitoring and assessment; behaviour management; and other topics related to the Standards and life in schools. The STCCs also work with the university partnership co-ordinator in preparing activities for the trainees.

Comments from head teachers and STCCs were sought on the new arrangements and were very positive:

> Staff don't see them [trainees] as a burden . . . they haven't parachuted in here for a few days and then disappeared . . . they have become part of the school, so we have got more ownership. (head teacher)

> I think the strength is . . . we have a clear picture of the whole year, of how many students we have and what the tasks entail, whereas in the past we were looking on a term by term basis. (head teacher)

> We've been involved from the outset . . . you [the university] gave us some basic guidelines as to what we should be doing with the trainees in seminars, you're giving us responsibility and recognising that we will do a good job. (STCC)

> Well, I think they [the trainees] see the school exactly as it is. There's nothing staged for them, they see the colours of the year, the autumns, the springs and the summers. They see the pressured times, they see the times when we have fun and celebrate. They get a whole range of experiences. (head teacher)

There are as many different partnership arrangements as there are training providers but you can be sure that the schools in which you are placed will have a very important part to play in your training.

## Different routes into teaching

Teaching is now an all-graduate profession. For most primary teachers the route to achieving Qualified Teaching Status (QTS) is an undergraduate one involving three or four years of study resulting in a Bachelor of Education degree (BEd), Bachelor of Arts in Education (BA(Ed)) or Bachelor of Science in Education (BSc(Ed)). These degrees are awarded with QTS. Another route is with a Postgraduate Certificate in Education (PGCE) with QTS following a first degree, and usually consists of a year of study at a university. PGCEs and degrees are awarded by Higher Education Institutions while QTS is awarded by the DfES through the General Teaching Council for England or Wales. The pathways described above are all university-based, but there are also employment-based routes into teaching. School Centred Initial Teacher Training (SCITT) programmes have been introduced where individual schools take on the full responsibility for an individual's training. Graduate and Registered Teacher Programmes (GTP and RTP) are also school-based routes where trainees receive their training in the school.

## Overview of this book

This chapter has provided you with a context for your teacher training. The following chapters will take you through the important theory and practice that you will need in order to meet QTS Standards and, in doing so, provide you with the knowledge, skills and understanding that will form the basis of your teaching. This book, with its theoretical underpinning, case studies and activities, will hopefully help you to reflect on all aspects of teaching and learning and question the many initiatives that will certainly come your way during your teaching career.

## Suggestions for further reading

This chapter has covered a wide range of ideas and initiatives but perhaps the most interesting is the recent focus on creativity in the primary classroom. *Creativity in the Primary Curriculum* by Jones and Wyse (2004) will give you some further ideas. It addresses creativity in all areas of the curriculum, giving a rationale for the introduction of more creativity in terms of learning, and also gives lots of practical ideas.

## References

Beard, R. (1999) *The National Literacy Strategy: Review of Research and Other Related Evidence*. London: DfEE.

Brown, M., Askew, M., Millett, A. and Rhodes, V. (2003) 'The key role of educational research in the development and evaluation of the National Numeracy Strategy'. *British Educational Research Journal*, **29**(5), October. 655–67.

Cajkler, W. (1999) 'Misconceptions in the NLS: National Literacy Strategy or No Linguistic Sense?', in *The Use of English*, **50**(3), 214–27.

Clarke, C. (2003) 'Foreword', in *Excellence and Enjoyment: A Strategy for Primary Schools*. Nottingham: DfES.

DES (1977) *Education in Schools*. London: HMSO.

DfEE (1998) *Teaching: High Status, High Standards (Circular 4/98). Requirements for Courses of Initial Teacher Training*. London: DfEE.

DfEE (1998a) *The National Literacy Strategy*. London: DfEE.

DfEE (1998b) *The National Numeracy Strategy*. London: DfEE.

DfEE/QCA (1999) *The National Curriculum: Handbook for Primary Teachers in England*. London: DfEE.

DfES (2003) *Excellence and Enjoyment: A Strategy for Primary Schools*. Nottingham: DfES.

DfES/QCA (2003) *Speaking, Listening, Learning: Working with Children in Key Stages 1 and 2*. London: DfES/QCA.

Early Years Curriculum Group (1998) *Interpreting the National Curriculum at Key Stage 1*. Buckingham: Open University Press.

Edwards, A. and Knight, P. (1994) *Effective Early Years Education*. Buckingham: Open University Press.

Edwards, T. (1995) 'The politics of partnership', in Bines, H. and Welton, J.M. (eds) *Managing Partnership in Teacher Training*. London: Routledge.

English, E., Hargreaves, L. and Hislam, J. (2003) 'Can we talk about that later?', in Moyles, J., Hargreaves, L., Merry, R., Paterson, F. and Escarte-Sarries, V. (eds) *Interactive Teaching in Primary Classrooms*. Maidenhead: Open University Press.

Jones, R. and Wyse, D. (2004) *Creativity in the Primary Curriculum*. London: David Fulton.

Newton. L. (1995) 'Diagnostic monitoring in a primary partnership', in Griffiths, G. and Owen, P. *Schools in Partnership*. London: Paul Chapman.

QCA/DfEE (2000) *Curriculum Guidance for the Foundation Stage*. London: QCA.

SCAA (1996) *Desirable Outcomes for Children's Learning on Entering Compulsory Education*. York: School Curriculum and Assessment Authority.

Stanovich, K. and Stanovich, P. (1995) 'How research might inform the debate about early reading acquisition'. *Journal of Research in Reading*, **18**(2), 87–105.

Wilkin, M. and Sankey, D. (1994) Editorial Introduction, in Wilkin, M. and Sankey, D. (eds) *Collaboration and Transition in Initial Teacher Training*. London: Kogan Page.

# The reflective practitioner

## Lynn Newton

## Introduction

An examination of the structure and content of any initial teacher training course reflects the complexity of the role of the teacher. Guidance documents often identify the reflective teaching model as underpinning the professional and pedagogical knowledge to be developed by trainees. In particular, you need to think about:

- your knowledge of yourself as teacher;
- your knowledge of the content (curriculum) to be covered;
- your knowledge of teaching and learning as processes;
- your knowledge of your pupils as individual learners; and
- your knowledge of the school and societal contexts in which you work.

## Activity 2.1

With these in mind, think of five reasons why you want to become a primary teacher, then classify your reasons as focused on: yourself; the children; the teaching content; some other reason.

These knowledge bases are seen as essential for any prospective teacher to acquire. They underpin a constructivist approach to teaching that emphasises the larger concepts, pupils' questioning strategies, co-operative activities and active participation. Creative problem-solving is seen as fundamental to a constructivist approach, with teachers assessing and solving problems by asking crucial questions about decision-making. Indeed, the Primary National Strategy (DfES 2003) emphasises this relationship.

## Teaching – a complex process

The complexity underpinning your role of teacher is seldom recognised. Try asking a few members of your family or friends what they think a teacher does when he or she is working in classrooms with five-year-olds or ten-year-olds. Capel *et al.* (1999: 10) did something like this and found, in their study of the general public, that the majority of people held the view that the teacher's role was a straightforward one of standing in front of the class and talking to them. This is, of course, a very simplistic view. Capel *et al.* go on to liken perceptions of the teacher's work to an iceberg; people see only the classroom practice, which represents 10 per cent of their work, the visible 'tip of the iceberg'. Like an iceberg, the other 90 per cent of what a teacher does is hidden from view. This comprises:

- the planning and preparation that goes on beforehand;
- the broad and deep subject and pedagogical knowledge the teacher needs to have;
- the personal skills and qualities he or she brings to the role;
- the skills of monitoring, assessment and evaluation needed;
- the establishment of routines and organisational structures; and
- the ability to exercise professional judgement.

This is the *real* teacher. When trainees go into the classroom for the first time, they sometimes comment on how easy their teachers make the job of teaching look. They see only the visible 10 per cent (like the general public); they have yet to appreciate the hidden 90 per cent that makes up the effective practitioner.

## Progression in becoming a teacher

So what are you really seeing when you see an effective teacher at work? You need to look beyond the readily visible at what it is that makes that teacher appear so effective. The characteristics of an effective teacher are discussed in detail by Douglas Newton in Chapter 4, 'Teaching and learning'. Freeman (1996) discusses three useful views of teaching:

1 as doing (the behaviourist view);
2 as thinking and doing (the cognitivist view); and
3 as knowing what to do (the interpretivist view).

The first view attempts to connect the teacher's actions to the pupils' learning. The second view sees skilled teaching as a combination of the mental activities of the teacher and visible behaviours of both the teacher and the pupils. The final view has the experienced and effective teacher interpreting available information and applying it in his or her own classroom, making decisions about how and why to act in particular ways and then carrying through these decisions.

You can see here the progression from the newly qualified teacher, who has skills but is relatively inexperienced, through to the experienced teacher and, ultimately, the expert teacher. Most trainees, when they begin their training, can be classed as novices. Your initial teacher training course will be designed to raise your awareness of the complexity of your role as a teacher. Your programmes will support you in the development of relevant subject and pedagogical knowledge. You will have opportunities on your school placements to practise relevant skills and to apply this knowledge. All these will be necessary for you to meet the government's requirements for initial teacher training, the Standards required for Qualified Teacher Status (QTS) (DfES 2002).

But even when your training course is finished you will not be an expert. You have only begun the process of Continuing Professional Development. Throughout your training programme, and even when you are a qualified teacher, you should be regularly asking yourself:

- How can I improve as a teacher?
- How can I progress as an effective practitioner?
- How do I continue my professional development?

Pollard *et al.* (2002) suggest that you need to develop the skills of reflecting on practice; that is, to become a reflective teacher. Indeed, he argues that all teachers can benefit from becoming reflective teachers. Bailey (1997: 1) makes a case for thinking about reflective teaching as a practice (a way of working); as an attitude (a way of thinking); as a way of being professional (a way of interacting); and as a source of potentially insightful solutions to problems (a way of reaching decisions).

What is important, whether you are a trainee new to the profession or a teacher with many years of experience, is to think about the activity in which you are engaged. What do you want to accomplish with your pupils? Why have you chosen those goals? How can you best achieve them? On your initial teacher training programme you will not complete your school placements successfully and gain QTS if you cannot teach, so the award of QTS indicates that you can do the job. You have the necessary skills and have reached at least a minimal level of competence. Is this enough? Those of us who have been teachers for a long time know that there are some teachers who have been teaching for many years but who can be described as having one year's experience many times over; they are competent teachers but they have stood still in their thinking and practices. On the other hand, other teachers have moved on. Many years of experience really should mean many years of thought, learning, change, adaptation and personal development. This emphasises that experience is a necessary, but insufficient, condition for professional development as a teacher. More is needed. In the government's proposals for Continuing Professional Development, one of their stated aims focuses on reflective teaching:

> We want to encourage teachers, as reflective practitioners, to think about what they do well, to reflect on what they could share with colleagues, as well as identifying their own learning needs. (DfEE 2001: 12)

This introduces the concept of the reflective practitioner. What does this mean? In the remainder of this chapter we will explore this idea and consider some of its implications for you.

## What is a reflective teacher?

The notion of the reflective practitioner is not new, nor is it applicable only to the teaching profession. There are many interpretations and models of reflective practice that are influential in the context of education, some of which will be discussed here.

Dewey (1933) discussed thinking and teaching, and contrasted bad thinking and routine teaching with reflective thought and reflective teaching. This is a distinction which Pollard *et al.* (2002) sees as fundamental to the concept of professional development. Routine teaching actions are guided by factors such as tradition and habit ('I do it like this because I have always done it like this . . .'), and authority ('. . . and it works'). They are, by their nature, static and unresponsive to change. This is the teacher who has been teaching for 20 years with one year's experience repeated 20 times over. Reflective action, on the other hand, indicates a social and educational awareness and a willingness to carry out self-evaluation and to acquire the necessary skills to develop and be flexible. For Dewey, a reflective experience involves:

1 a situation that is incomplete, resulting in confusion because the full picture is not yet obvious;

2 a tentative interpretation of what is known, with anticipation of effects or consequences;

3 a definition and clarification of the problem in hand through a careful analysis of all attainable considerations;

4 elaboration of a tentative hypothesis to fit with the known situation; and

5 testing the hypothesis by translating it into a plan of action and applying it in the current situation.

Elements 3 and 4 are the crucial components for reflective experience as opposed to trial-and-error experiences. According to Dewey it is the thinking itself – indeed the quality thinking – that is an experience. At the heart of the model is a cyclical process that leads to the construction of meaning. This happens when:

**1** awareness is created by observation (noticing things) and gathering information (collecting data and other evidence);

**2** the information (data and evidence) is analysed to identify implications;

**3** a tentative hypothesis (idea) is suggested, based on the observations and evidence, to explain events and guide further actions; and

**4** a plan is devised and acted upon.

Another influential writer on reflective practice is Donald Schön (1983). His analysis of reflective practice is summed up well by Pollard (2002). Schön suggests that as teachers we should engage in 'reflection-in-action'. This means that we adjust our teaching in line with the feedback we receive from our pupils. We do not separate thinking from action. He also suggests that teachers also engage in the process he calls 'reflection-*on*-action'. This occurs not only when we think about what we are going to do but also when, afterwards, we think about what we have done, and especially when we share this thinking with colleagues who advise and help us improve (Zeichner and Liston 1996).

You should have noticed the emphasis on the relationship between theory and practice. For Bartlett (1990), reflection is the key to integrating practice and theory – the 'know what' and 'know how' with the 'know why'. The process of reflection should, according to Bartlett, be aimed at becoming a *critically* reflective teacher by immersion in the wider context of teaching. This brings in the idea of values and goals and gives meaning to questioning issues and initiatives. Bartlett distinguishes between 'how to' questions (directly related to the methodology of teaching) and 'what/why' questions (making decisions by reflecting upon the issues). Knowledge is crucial in this process of reflecting on issues. It follows that as you progress from novice to expert, using Bartlett's model, you should move from the 'how' questions towards the 'what/why' questions, with reflection operating as the mechanism to achieve this shift. There will be a transition from collective information about teaching as a process to a conscious and critical examination of the attitudes and beliefs that underpin that teaching.

You will notice that there is, once again, an emphasis on *critical* reflection. This crucial component is related to how you, as the teacher, think about and use (or challenge) the body of knowledge that the teaching profession recognises and promotes as valuable (aims and objectives, strategies and approaches, or content and curriculum). This is likely to be that which is passed on to you in your initial training programme and early career. This can be compared to the often intuitive and tacit knowledge of teaching and learning that you, as a teacher, will develop through experience. Think back to the earlier comment about the two teachers who had both been teaching for 20 years, but only one had 20 years' experience because of this critical reflection.

In essence, skilled reflective teachers are teachers who consistently examine their values and beliefs, attitudes and assumptions, and teaching practices. They use their insights to improve their teaching. It could be argued that these are also the qualities of an effective teacher. The difference is in the extent to which the reflective practitioner is willing and able to collect data (information) and to use this as the basis for *critical* reflection.

## Making reflective teaching a reality

To become this critical reflective thinker, according to Dewey (1933) you will need three key attitudes:

1 open-mindedness
2 responsibility
3 whole-heartedness.

### Activity 2.2

1 Think back to your own school experiences (primary or secondary). Who were the teachers who had the greatest influence on you? Did they exhibit these qualities? Did these qualities affect you in ways other than the classroom learning experience?

2 How can this awareness help you as a prospective primary teacher? How is your own training programme preparing you to be the kind of teacher who questions:
   - education goals and values;
   - the classroom and school contexts;
   - the curriculum; and
   - instructional strategies.

Pollard *et al.* (2002) state that reflective teachers exhibit six crucial characteristics. They:

1 have an active concern with aims and consequences, as well as means and technical efficiency;

2 monitor, evaluate and revise their own practice continuously through a cyclical process;

3 support the development of teaching competence through their competence in methods of classroom enquiry;

4 have attitudes of open-mindedness, responsibility and whole-heartedness;

5 draw on self-reflection and insights from the educational disciplines to make judgements; and

6 enhance professional learning and personal fulfilment through collaboration and dialogue with colleagues.

These various characteristics or stages come together in a cyclical process, comprising a series of steps or stages.

## Challenges facing the primary teacher

In the government's 1985 science policy statement, ten criteria for good practice are identified (DES 1985). Although prescribed in the context of science, they are of relevance to any teacher who is teaching any curriculum area. These follow.

### 1. Breadth

All pupils should experience a curriculum offering a breadth of skills, knowledge and understanding. Most National Curriculum areas of experience are designed to reflect this breadth in their Programmes of Study. But, of course, there is scope to go beyond the National Curriculum.

### 2. Balance

Pupils will be taught by a variety of teachers with different levels of expertise in different subject areas. It is sometimes tempting to miss things out and leave it to another teacher to deal with, or to spend longer than is reasonable on, an area because it happens to be an area that either you do not like or you are enthusiastic about. This would deny pupils a balance in their curricular experiences.

### 3. Relevance

Children need to appreciate why their learning experiences are as they are, why learning is important, initially to them as individuals and later to the society in which they will live and work as adults. By making the relevance of learning experiences explicit, teachers can help children value the learning process and, hopefully, become independent learners.

### 4. Differentiation

In essence, the mental and physical demands of any learning experience should be matched to the needs and abilities of the learners. These need to be taken into account when planning any experience.

### 5. Equal opportunities

Every child in the class has a right to access the experiences on offer, regardless of their sex, race or ability and, furthermore, to make progress as a result of the experiences provided.

### 6. Continuity

Children usually spend seven years in a primary school. There needs to be continuity in the planning of experiences so that each year builds upon what has gone before and lays foundations for what is to follow.

## 7. Progression

As well as continuity in the curriculum, there is progression in the children's learning and the two must be reconciled. Knowing where children are starting from – their prior learning and experiences – provides the baseline for the current experience and the construction of new understandings.

## 8. Links across the curriculum

Young children do not compartmentalise learning experiences into subject areas; that is something adults do for their organisational convenience. Yet young children quickly learn the divisions of mathematics or history or music. Cross-curricular opportunities, however, can more realistically reflect the real world and be more meaningful and relevant.

## 9. Teaching methods and approaches

The key here is variety. No single method or approach works for everything. Whether it is whole-class teaching, as opposed to group work, or practical activities, as opposed to watching a video, each can have its place for a justified purpose.

## 10. Assessment

The process of assessment goes hand-in-hand with monitoring progress, keeping records for different purposes and giving feedback to different audiences. Different methods of assessment for different purposes need to be used.

As the role of the primary teacher is so complex, there will be a number of challenges that you will have to face as a teacher. These are to do with:

- *organisation* – of children, other adults, resources, tasks, space, time;
- *interaction* – relating to children, staff, parents, other adults;
- *delegation/control* – how much freedom to give, what limits to set, flexibility;
- *motivation* – children's involvement, relevance, expectations;
- *standards* – quality control, breadth, balance, progression;
- *individual needs* – differentiation, individual programmes, special needs;
- *National Curriculum* – integration, subject teaching, time on each area; and
- *whole-curriculum issues* – personal/social/moral development, equality.

This means that, to prove your competence, you must rise to the challenge, reconcile numerous demands and make numerous decisions. To resolve the dilemmas you must use your professional judgement to assess the situation, make decisions on how to act and have the skills to carry out those actions. If you do so effectively, you will be exhibiting the characteristics of the next level of competent practitioner – the experienced and reflective teacher. As such, you go through a cycle of reflective teaching: planning action, organising for action, carrying it out, collecting evidence of the consequences, analysing and evaluating evidence, reflecting upon it and feeding that reflection into the next planning cycle.

Pollard *et al.* (2002: 4) discuss how the process of reflection 'feeds a constructive spiral of professional development and capability'. This capability – or skills and professional competence – develops with time, opportunity, experience and reflection. In your teaching career you will exhibit different levels of competence as you travel along the route from *novice* (the student teacher at the beginning of your training), through *competent* (the new teacher in the first few years of teaching) to *expert* (the teacher who is thoughtful, adaptable, searching for ways to move the teaching and learning forward). When you finish your course you take with you your career entry and development profile. This identifies your experiences during training, your particular strengths and areas for further development. During your induction year you will be supported both within the school (by the head teacher or a designated mentor) and by the LEA with a programme aimed at meeting your personal development needs. This support should help you deal with the challenges of classroom life. It is these challenges and how you deal with them that identifies the stage of your development from novice to expert. You will need to be able to recognise the range of issues; identify which of those issues are important; understand the situation as a whole; and make appropriate decisions. You should be able to see that your professional development as a teacher is a continuous process that will enable you to acquire the skills, knowledge and understanding to do this. Remember that you cannot stand still; children, curricula and environments all change. You must be flexible and adapt to change. You must be a reflective practitioner.

## Activity 2.3

Construct your own competence action plan. Think of your own development as a primary teacher:

(a) What level of competence do you bring to the start of your teaching career?

(b) What are your weaknesses as far as teaching the full primary curriculum is concerned?

(c) If given a free choice in your first three years of teaching, what continuing professional development support or courses would you like to participate in to address your weaknesses or develop your competence further?

(d) Draw up a personal action plan, outlining a timescale for what you would like to achieve and how you might achieve it.

A good starting point is to begin a 'Reflective Journal'. As often as possible, and ideally after each teaching day, write about your experience. Try to reflect upon the strategies you use for setting the scene, the tone of the lesson, establishing expectations, communicating ideas and gaining your pupils' respect. Also think about how you developed your own expertise, whether through reading and research or discussions with colleagues.

In the case study that follows, think about the conceptions of teaching represented, the progression of the teacher from novice to experienced to expert, and the steps in the cycle of reflective practice discussed.

## Case study 2.1: Marla

I currently teach a Year 4 class in a large suburban primary school in the north of England. I have been at this school for eight years. Before that I taught for five years in an infant school in Leicestershire and then was a science co-ordinator in an inner-city primary school in Leicester for three years with a Year 5 class.

Even though I did a PGCE, following my degree in biochemistry, I don't think anything on my training course really prepared me for the complexity of my role as it is now. I don't recall hearing or reading anything about reflective practice. It wasn't until I did a diploma module that I came across that idea, and it made absolute sense. I wish I had discovered it sooner!

During teaching practices I remember doing everything by the book. I planned everything in great detail, wrote absolutely everything down and accepted everything I was told. As a novice teacher, faced with a large class, I felt lacking in the necessary professional resources – intellectual as well as physical – to do anything apart from just cope. The solution lay in keeping my pupils busy, finding the right resources for them to use and keeping on top of the discipline. I didn't question anything. It wasn't just that I didn't have time to challenge things; it was more that I didn't have the confidence or the know-how to feel sure of my ground. That came later and is partly the result of experience, but also of reading and thinking about what I do and why I do it. I have some interesting debates with my colleagues, especially the head. He calls me argumentative at times, but it's really more about wanting to understand why things are the way they are and what I can do about changing things if I believe there are alternatives.

For example, at the moment, as both the deputy head teacher and the science co-ordinator, I'm fighting a real battle about the place of science in the primary curriculum. It has been marginalised in my school because of the push for the literacy and numeracy hours. At school meetings I try to explain to other staff, governors, parents and anyone who will listen what science is and why it is important. From talking to colleagues from other schools, at meetings, I don't believe this situation is unique. But that doesn't make it right. Science is a core area and should be given more time. I value it and I feel my colleagues should do the same.

If I had to give today's student teachers a piece of advice it would be to take very seriously the evaluations they do. Planning is very important but evaluation is equally important, and this isn't stressed enough. Evaluation isn't just that the lesson went well, the plan worked and the children enjoyed it; it is about: Why did the lesson go well? What did I do that made it effective? Can I do that again or should I modify it in some way? Why was the plan successful? What goals were achieved? Did all the children enjoy it? How do I know? What about Jane Shaw who was absent? Did Rashid really understand the bit about perimeter? How do I know? Is this the best way to do this? The questions are endless, but it is this self-questioning, this reflection, that is so important. And the more they think and read and talk to experienced colleagues, the better will they be able to answer these questions.

I would also add a second piece of advice: once they start teaching they should go on every in-service course they can. Talking with other colleagues, sharing ideas and picking up tips are all about moving forward as a teacher.

## Suggestions for further reading

If you would like to explore some of the issues touched upon in this chapter, the following books should be of interest to you:

Ghaye, A. and Ghaye, K. (1998) *Teaching and Learning through Critical Reflective Practice*. London: David Fulton Publishers.

This book provides an overview of the nature and purposes of reflective practice and evaluates the claims being made for it. It takes a holistic model of the teacher as a reflective practitioner and explores the ten principles that underpin this model.

Pollard, A. (ed.) (2002) *Readings for Reflective Teaching*. London: Continuum.

In this weighty book Andrew Pollard brings together readings from experts in education across the whole spectrum of educational pedagogy. He does not limit himself to contemporary writers but includes writings from the past to show how ideas in education have changed and developed. The whole is intended to support the primary teacher in the process of reflecting on his or her own practice.

Pollard, A., Collins, J., Simco, N. *et al.* (2002) *Reflective Teaching: Effective and Evidence-informed Professional Practice*. London: Continuum.

This is a companion volume to *Readings for Reflective Teaching* but is much more focused on actual classroom practice, supporting the student teacher and the new practitioner. Again, it is a large volume that covers a wide range of educational skills and ideas. Pollard's books are supported by a website (*RTweb*), providing free resources to support reflective classroom practice, that is updated termly by the editors. It can be accessed via *http://www.rtweb.info*.

## References

Bailey, K.M. (1997) 'Reflective teaching: situating our stories'. *Asian Journal of English Language Teaching*, **7**, 1–19.

Bartlett, L. (1990) 'Teacher development through reflective teaching', in J.C. Richards and D. Nunan (eds) *Second Language Teacher Education*. Cambridge: Cambridge University Press, pp. 202–14.

Capel, S., Leask, M. and Turner, T. (1999) *Learning to Teach in the Secondary School: A Companion to School Experience* (2nd edn). London: Routledge, Section 5.4: 'Improving your teaching: an introduction to action research and reflective practice', pp. 276–82.

DES (1985) *Science 5–16: A Statement of Policy*. London: HMSO.

Dewey, J. (1933) *How We Think: A Restatement of the Relation of Reflective Thinking to the Educative Process.* Chicago: Henry Regnery.

DfEE (2001) *Continuing Professional Development*. London: DfEE.

DfES (2002) *Qualifying to Teach: Professional Standards for Qualified Teacher Status and Requirements for Initial Teacher Training* (Circular 02/02). London: DfES.

DfES (2003) *Excellence and Enjoyment: A Strategy for Primary Schools*. Nottingham: DfES.

Freeman, D. (1996) 'Redefining the relationship between research and what teachers know', in K.M. Bailey and D. Nunan (eds) *Voices from the Language Classroom*. Cambridge: Cambridge University Press, pp. 88–115.

Pollard, A., Collins, J., Simco, N. *et al.* (2002) *Reflective Teaching: Effective and Evidence-informed Professional Practice*. London: Continuum.

Schön, D.A. (1983) *The Reflective Practitioner: How Professionals Think in Action*. New York: Basic Books.

Zeichner, K.M. and Liston, D.P. (1996) *Reflective Teaching: An Introduction*. Mahwah, NJ: Lawrence Erlbaum Associates.

# Teachers and the law

Lynn Newton

## Introduction

The aim of this chapter is to raise your awareness of some aspects of the law that are relevant to teachers. It does not cover everything and is not intended to be a legal guide or a source of advice on legal matters. Should you want or need further information on the matters discussed, or other such matters, you should consult a legal expert.

Being a teacher is a huge responsibility and not one to be taken lightly. As a primary teacher, for 12 months you will be a significant influence on the development of a group of young people. You will be responsible for meeting not only their intellectual needs, but in many cases their social and emotional needs, and occasionally their physical needs. You have a duty of care and need to be alert to your statutory responsibilities as well as your legal liabilities as a teacher. In order to carry out your professional responsibilities alongside your various educative roles, you need to behave as any reasonable and responsible parent or adult would. You are also expected to respond as a trained professional. Teaching is a regulated profession; acts of parliament, codes of practice, custom and precedent all determine how we can and should behave. However, what counts as reasonable is subject to the vagaries of a changing society and issues are seldom clear-cut.

## Fitness to teach

So where do you begin to untangle this complexity? The starting point for ensuring that *you* are an appropriate person to have the care of and responsibility for children is to be given clearance by the Criminal Records Bureau (CRB). This is the body that provides checks on criminal backgrounds and verifies that the checks have been carried out and that you have no serious criminal convictions that prohibit you from working with children. Before you start your training you will also have had a health check to verify that you are mentally and physically fit to teach. These would be two of the many requirements that you will have had to meet before commencing your training.

# The General Teaching Councils

Once on the course, other legal issues will have been raised and discussed with you in order that you can fulfil your role as teacher. One of the standards in *Qualifying to Teach* (TTA 2002, Standard 1.8) requires that anyone who is awarded Qualified Teacher Status (QTS) must understand and uphold the professional code of the General Teaching Council (GTC) for England. Scotland has had a General Teaching Council (GTCS) since 1965, but it was not until 2000 that similar bodies for England (GTCE) and for Wales (GTCW) were established. On taking up a position in a state-funded school you are required to be a member of the relevant GTC. The councils play a major role in defining professional conduct and practice (see, for example, the *Code of Professional Values and Practice for Teachers*, GTCE 2002).

The GTCs have been given the powers, through the Disciplinary Functions Regulations, to investigate professional conduct and competence (or, more significantly, professional misconduct and incompetence) and to terminate a teacher's registration as a qualified teacher. Yet the government, through the Secretary of State, retains major powers over entry to the profession, teachers' pay and conditions of service and, of course, through its various bills, acts and laws, the government steers the general direction of education.

This all sounds rather daunting, yet these codes of conduct and legal frameworks are important, not only for the protection of the children but also for your own protection. You are not expected to have a detailed knowledge of the whole legal framework; rather, you need to be aware of your own statutory rights *and* responsibilities, both as a teacher and as an employee. These will help you to handle day-to-day situations efficiently and effectively. You should also know where to turn for more information should you need it.

## Rights and responsibilities

From the outset you need to be familiar with the main rights and responsibilities of a primary teacher. You should also be aware of key legislation which impinges upon a teacher's work and should explore how to deal with situations so that you can anticipate and avoid problems.

### Activity 3.1

Think about how you might deal with:

- a fight in the playground while you are on duty;
- a child who, while changing for PE, shows signs of physical abuse;
- a child who wants to be cuddled;
- a child with a nose bleed.

Review your answers once you have familiarised yourself with the appropriate codes of conduct and relevant legislation.

## Your rights as a teacher

As a teacher, you have the same rights as any other employee in any other job. All schools, whether state-funded (maintained) or independent (private) must abide by general UK legislation on employment and anti-discrimination. Whether you work full-time or part-time, your employer must:

- respect your human rights (Human Rights Act 1998, 2001);
- treat you fairly and equally regardless of sex, race, marital status, disability, or membership of a trade union (the Sex Discrimination Act 1975; the Disability Discrimination Act 1995, 2002; and the Race Relations Act 1976, 2000); and
- ensure you have a healthy, safe environment in which to work (Health and Safety at Work Act 1974).

You will be issued with a contract of employment and will have an agreed salary, both of which are controlled by various articles of contract law and the annually updated *School Teachers' Pay and Conditions of Service* document (HMSO 1987, 1991 amendment) which applies to all teachers employed in maintained schools. There are also clear regulations and requirements about your right to leave (for example in connection with adoption, maternity or paternity leave and parental leave, or time away to care for dependants) and in connection with disciplinary or redundancy procedures.

You are strongly advised to join one of the teachers' unions, usually free to trainees. This will give you access to advice and expertise, provide insurance and a legal framework to protect you should something go wrong, and protect you against unfair treatment in your employment and in your career.

## Your responsibilities as a teacher

When I first started teaching, a colleague with many years of experience told me that her golden rule in her classroom was 'Employ the three Cs – Care, Courtesy and Common Sense'. This is not a bad rule from which to view your duties and responsibilities as a teacher.

You have obvious contractual duties connected with your conditions of employment (as defined in the current *School Teachers' Pay and Conditions of Service* document). There are different sets of conditions for particular staff (for example, head teachers and advanced skills teachers). There are also conditions that apply to all teachers other than head teachers. You will be expected to fulfil these duties under the direction of the head teacher and other senior staff, and you are likely to have a mentor who should induct you into these codes and procedures. In addition, there will be a school governing body. According to Hyland (2003), the governing body has a central role in the overall direction of the school. Staff appointments and the disciplining of staff, the aims of the school and development of policies, admission procedures and budgets – all are determined by the governing body collectively.

Although the list is, potentially, endless, your responsibilities as a teacher are likely to include:

- planning for teaching and learning;

- meeting curriculum requirements;

- monitoring and assessing progress;

- maintaining records and reporting on progress;

- promoting children's all-round development and wellbeing;

- observing the SEN code of practice;

- maintaining discipline and good order; and

- creating and maintaining a safe and secure learning environment.

All of these are of direct relevance to what goes on with pupils in your classroom and around the school. There are also other activities. For example, you are likely to be required to:

- attend assemblies (unless there is an accepted reason for not doing so, for example, religious grounds);

- register and monitor attendance, and supervise pupils (for example, at the start and end of the day and at break times);

- participate in quality assurance and appraisal procedures (for example, Ofsted);

- attend staff meetings and staff development days;

- prepare for and participate in external examinations procedures (such as the National Tests); and

- participate in the school's behaviour management procedures which may involve, for example, after-school detention.

As you will see, your duties as a teacher extend beyond teaching your pupils in your classroom. It would be very easy for workloads to increase unreasonably, and with this in mind there has been a recent review of teachers' workloads and responsibilities. A report to the government's School Teachers' Review Body (STRB) resulted in the publication of proposals for dealing with excessive workloads, giving teachers more time to focus on teaching and increased administrative support to carry out their roles (DfES 2002).

## Health and safety matters

The health and safety legislation is complex but it applies to schools in the same way as it applies to factories, offices and other places of work. Usually the local education authority or the governing body will be responsible for the overall written health and safety policy. There will be someone in your school (usually the head teacher) who is the health and safety officer. He or she will have been on training programmes in connection with this and is responsible for the day-to-day implementation of the policy. However, it will be your responsibility to make yourself familiar with the safety policy and apply it in your classroom with your pupils. The policy will cover matters like:

- emergency procedures (fire drills, etc.);

- accidents (reporting procedures, medical facilities, etc.);

- school security (generally, intruders, abusive or threatening visitors, etc.);

- equipment (electrical, PE, science, etc.); and

- school visits (organisation, permissions, staffing, etc.).

Subject co-ordinators (or curriculum area leaders) are likely to have produced documents that interpret the general policies for specific contexts and, once again, you need to familiarise yourself with these and act on them. If in doubt, ask for advice. You should carry out mental 'risk assessments' of situations and take reasonable precautions to avoid being accused of lack of care or negligence.

For some activities you may want to do, this is not just important, but crucial. For example, it is quite likely you will want to take your class on a school trip. You will need to ensure that the children are appropriately supervised and not exposed to dangers. There are government and union guidelines on school trips that have usually been used by local education authorities and schools to create their own guidelines and policies. It is these that should be the starting point for your own planning.

You should then be able to identify, for example:

- the individual roles and responsibilities of everyone who is to be involved;

- the sequence of tasks to be completed prior to the visit;

- the necessary risk assessments and safety audits to be completed;

- the permissions needed;

- any insurance cover needed;

- the ratio of teachers to pupils required; and

- the constraints on the involvement of other adults.

This list is by no means complete, since individual policies vary. Union advice on school trips is that staff involvement is entirely voluntary unless the visit is part of a curriculum programme.

## Your duty of care and the children's rights

The Children Act (1989) lays on you a duty of care with respect to the children you are working with. In all of the situations in which you will work as a teacher you must remember that the children have human rights; they have a right to be in a safe environment, and the disability and discrimination legislation applies to them in the same way as it applies to you. The schools you work in will have an equal opportunities policy that you must follow. Reasonable steps must be taken to ensure that no pupil is disadvantaged because of sex, race or disability. Access to curricular experiences, resources and facilities must be planned with this in mind.

Obviously, the Children Act is primarily concerned with protecting children from harm and, particularly, from any kind of abuse or neglect. In your work as a teacher, your day-to-day contact with children means that you can play a positive role in child protection by spotting signs of possible abuse. You are also vulnerable to accusations of abuse. Abuse is defined in the DfEE (1995) Circular 10/95, *Protecting Children from Abuse: The Role of the Education Service*, as:

- neglect (which is persistent and severe);

- physical injury (including potential injury) or failure to prevent injury or suffering; and

- emotional abuse (including persistent or severe emotional ill-treatment and rejection) which adversely affects the child's emotional and behavioural development.

All schools must have a child protection policy and a person designated to liaise with the statutory authorities. You must make yourself familiar with the procedures enshrined in the policy. However, as a teacher, it is not your responsibility to investigate or assess reports of abuse. You are legally required to treat confidentially and to report any incidents of suspected child abuse, in the first instance to your head teacher (or the person in the school who has been designated as responsible for child protection matters). He or she will then follow the required procedure, which usually involves contacting social services and the police.

You will be considered to have exercised your duty of care towards your pupils if you can demonstrate that you have behaved as any reasonable parent would have done. However, your responsibility goes beyond this because of the Children Act (1989), which requires of anyone with the care of children to do all that is reasonable under the circumstances to safeguard or promote the welfare of the child.

One of the major issues for any teacher concerns physical contact with children. Circular 10/95 (DfEE 1995) provides guidance for teachers, and LEAs and schools are likely to have produced their own guidelines. The law does not actually prohibit physical contact between a pupil and a teacher. You need to combine a commonsense approach with professional judgement. There may be circumstances where this is allowable, for example, for reassurance if a young child is injured or distressed. Remember, though, that pupils might misinterpret physical contact, even if accidental, and you must be aware of the limits and always err on the side of caution. How and where a child is touched is important and any inappropriate or indecent contact is inexcusable. As a teacher you must be sensitive to this.

Another form of physical contact is in connection with disciplining and/or restraining pupils. Schools must have a discipline policy, set by the governing body and implemented by the head teacher. Schools must also have a policy on bullying, which is defined as: 'deliberately hurtful behaviour, repeated over a period of time, where it is difficult for those being bullied to defend themselves' (Circular 10/95, DfEE 1995: 11).

The main types of bullying include: physical bullying (hitting, kicking, theft of property); verbal bullying (name-calling, racist remarks); and indirect bullying (social exclusion, spreading rumours). Teachers cannot ignore bullying; it is a form of abuse and must be taken seriously.

If it is necessary for you to intervene, it is not true that teachers can only use force in an emergency. Indeed, failure to take appropriate action may be as serious as intervening inappropriately. The 1996 Education Act enables teachers to intervene and use reasonable force (as defined by circumstances) when the purpose is to prevent a pupil from:

- committing an offence (including doing something that would be an offence if the pupil was not under the age of criminal responsibility);
- causing personal injury to themselves or someone else, including to property; and
- engaging in behaviour prejudicial to the maintenance of good order and discipline.

Each individual situation has to be evaluated to decide whether forceful intervention is appropriate and what the nature of that intervention should be. Guidance from unions suggests a range of things you might do. Factors that have to be borne in mind include the age of the pupil, whether more than one is involved and whether there is a physical object being used as a weapon. Will you or other pupils be at risk of injury? Should you seek help from another adult? Perhaps all that is needed is for you to block a pupil's path or put yourself between two pupils. Leading a pupil away from a situation by taking his or her hand or arm, or placing a hand in the small of the back, might be necessary. Sometimes something more forceful, like holding a pupil or pulling them aside, might be needed.

Under the 1996 Education Act, teachers are also allowed to detain pupils after school, providing certain conditions are met. It must have been generally made known by the head teacher to both pupils and parents that detention might be imposed and the latter must be given at least 24 hours' notice. Only a teacher authorised to do so may give detention and it must be in a form and of a duration that is considered reasonable in the circumstances. In all cases of disciplining pupils, teachers must be aware of, and follow carefully, the school policy on discipline and any associated guidance documents.

## Special educational needs (SEN)

Some pupils in your class may have been identified as having special educational needs, under the SEN Code of Practice (DfEE 1993; amended DfES 2001). You would still be responsible for these pupils, as their class teacher, and would need to plan for and deliver individualised programmes to meet their specific needs. The SEN Code of Practice provides guidance as to what you should do as a teacher in this situation. Your first port of call will normally be the SEN co-ordinator (SENCO) in your school. Together, you should plan and institute support structures for pupils who have been identified as having special educational needs and interventions to supplement those usually provided by the school.

## And if something goes wrong . . .?

Turner and Lofthouse (1995) provide a useful plan of action for helping you work through problems if they arise. In essence, they advise, if something happens:

1  *Don't panic* – stay calm and try to look calm even if you don't feel calm!

2  *Respond to it* – promptly and professionally deal with the situation by applying the codes of practice and procedures applicable.

3  *Record it* – once the incident is over, as soon as possible write down all the facts: time, place, people, context.

4  *Communicate* – inform your head teacher or other relevant staff about the incident who will advise you on how to proceed.

5  *Seek professional advice* – in the unlikely event of the incident becoming the subject of legal proceedings, pass it on to a lawyer – your LEA or union will advise on this.

Thankfully, such events are rare, but it is still better to be prepared. It is also important to note that all teachers, no matter how much experience they have, worry about such accidents and incidents. It is right to be professionally concerned but you should try to avoid being over-anxious. For Turner and Lofthouse (1995: 245) 'misfortunes often arise from what teachers have *not* done. The fundamental rules are:

1  Familiarise yourself with school policies and follow the rules and regulations carefully.

2  If in doubt about something, seek advice from colleagues in school or your union representative.

3  Avoid placing yourself in compromising situations (for example, if you are disciplining a child, ask a colleague to be present; avoid being alone with individual children other than in places that are in public view; carry out regular safety audits of activities and experiences).

### Activity 3.2

Take opportunities when you are in school to familiarise yourself with the nature and variety of official and legal documents that are in the school. Try to link the legislation to specific contexts (for example, how does the Health and Safety at Work Act (1974) relate to activities in PE, science, or design & technology?).

Look also for LEA or other guidelines that might be available for support.

## Case study 3.1: Meg

I've been teaching years . . . I trained in the seventies and, apart from a couple of short breaks, have taught full-time in a few different schools.

When I started it all seemed straightforward. As far as the law was concerned, at college *in loco parentis* was drummed into us. As long as we behaved as would reasonable, caring parents then that was all that mattered. We had some sessions on the history of education which gave us information on the key education acts and the main reports – especially the Plowden Report from the 1960s – but there wasn't much else.

Now we have legislation to deal with at every turn. If it's not to do with our job as teachers it's to do with our job as policemen or social workers or health visitors. Sometimes I think that the main job of educating children has got lost.

Not that I'm saying it's not appropriate – it's just that there's so much to think about. And I do think that it is important that we protect children from people like abusers, so I think it is important that students know about the law that applies to schools before they start.

## Suggestions for further reading

If you would like to explore some of the issues touched upon in this chapter, the following should be of interest to you:

Nixon, J. (2002) 'Schoolteachers' conditions of service', in M. Cole (ed.), *Professional Values and Practice for Teachers and Student Teachers*. London: David Fulton Publishers, chapter 8, pp. 99–123.

Nixon, J. (2002) 'Schoolteachers' legal liabilities and responsibilities', in M. Cole (ed.), *Professional Values and Practice for Teachers and Student Teachers*. London: David Fulton Publishers, chapter 9, pp. 124–43.

These two chapters by Jeff Nixon in Mike Cole's book provide a good summary of what you need to know as a teacher about your roles, responsibilities and rights.

Turner, D. and Lofthouse, M. (1995) 'Don't make a drama out of a crisis! Primary teachers and the law', in *Beginning Teaching: Beginning Learning in Primary Education*. Buckingham: Open University Press, chapter 15, pp. 244–55.

This chapter provides and excellent overview of educational legislation and the different aspects of civil and criminal law that applies in educational contexts. Case studies of real incidents are used to exemplify the issues discussed.

A range of documents that provide guidance on the matters discussed in this chapter can be found on the DfES website at: www.dfes.gov.uk/publications/guidanceonthe law/

In addition, you should look at the websites for some of the teacher unions. For example, National Union of Teachers (NUT) website can be found at: www.teachers.org.uk

## References

Hyland, R. (2003) 'Teachers' legal liabilities and statutory responsibilities', in K. Jacques and R. Hyland (eds) *Achieving QTS: Professional Studies – Primary Phase* (2nd edn). Exeter: Learning Matters, Chapter 14, pp. 172–82.

Turner, D. and Lofthouse, M. (1995) 'Don't make a drama out of a crisis! Primary teachers and the law', in Moyles, J. and Robinson, G. *Beginning Teaching: Beginning Learning in Primary Education*. Buckingham: Open University Press, chapter 15, pp. 244–55.

## Codes of practice, acts and official guidance

Commission for Racial Equality (CRE) (n.d.) *Code of Practice for the Elimination of Racial Discrimination in Education*. CRE website: www.cre.gov.uk

Department for Education and Employment (DfEE) (1993) *SEN Code of Practice*. London: HMSO.

Department for Education and Employment (DfEE) (1995) *Protecting Children from Abuse: The Role of the Education Service*. London: HMSO.

Department for Education and Skills (DfES) (2000) *Don't Suffer in Silence: An Anti-Bullying Pack for Schools*. London: DfES/HMSO.

Department for Education and Skills (DfES) (2001) *SEN Code of Practice (Amended)*. London: HMSO.

Department for Education and Skills (DfES) (2002) *Department for Education and Skills Response to STRB Workload Report*. London: DfES/HMSO.

General Teaching Council for England (GTCE) (2002) *Code of Professional Values and Practice for Teachers*. London: GTCE; GTCE website: http://www.gtce.org.uk/

Her Majesty's Stationery Office (HMSO) (1974) *The Health and Safety at Work Act*. London: HMSO.

Her Majesty's Stationery Office (HMSO) (1975) *The Sex Discrimination Act*. London: HMSO.

Her Majesty's Stationery Office (HMSO) (1976) *The Race Relations Act*. London: HMSO.

Her Majesty's Stationery Office (HMSO) (1987) *The Teachers' Pay and Conditions of Service Act*. London: HMSO.

Her Majesty's Stationery Office (HMSO) (1988) *The Education Reform Act*. London: HMSO.

Her Majesty's Stationery Office (HMSO) (1989) *The Children Act*. London: HMSO.

Her Majesty's Stationery Office (HMSO) (1991) *The School Teachers' Pay and Conditions Act*. London: HMSO.

Her Majesty's Stationery Office (HMSO) (1995) *The Disability Discrimination Act*. London: HMSO.

Her Majesty's Stationery Office (HMSO) (1998, 2001) *The Human Rights Act*. London: HMSO.

Her Majesty's Stationery Office (HMSO) (2000) *The Race Relations (Amendment) Act*. London: HMSO.

Her Majesty's Stationery Office (HMSO) (2001) *The Special Educational Needs and Disability Act*. London: HMSO.

Teacher Training Agency (TTA) (2002) *Qualifying to Teach: Professional Standards for Qualified Teacher Status and Requirements for Initial Teacher Training*. London: TTA.

# Teaching and learning in the primary school

Douglas P. Newton

## Introduction: expert teachers

Since you want to teach, I can probably assume that you want to teach well, that you want to make a difference, and that you want to become an expert at your job. There is a tendency to teach in much the same way as you were taught (Moallem 1998). If you were lucky enough to have an effective, expert teacher, that may not be a bad thing, but you have to remember that your teachers were probably trained many years ago. Expectations change, and some teachers are more expert than others. So what is it that makes an expert teacher?

First, expert teachers understand what they have to teach. This helps them have clear aims and keep their lessons on track. Second, they plan their lessons but can also change an approach in action if that is likely to produce better learning. They are also good at establishing routines that make things run smoothly, minimise potentially disruptive changes and ensure the children know what to do. They can look at a class, anticipate a problem and prevent it becoming one. Third, while teaching, they interact a lot with the children by, for instance, asking questions and drawing everyone into the learning process. But they do not pursue shallow learning, memorised facts and the regurgitation of their own words. When facts are important, as they are at times, they insist that they are learned but they do not leave it there; they also press for a deeper learning that involves understanding and knowing reasons. The children in their classes are more likely to be able to answer the question 'Why?' than children in classes where knowing 'What?' is the sole aim. Fourth, they monitor learning and provide feedback that helps children improve. They often appear to do this almost automatically, as in the way we come to drive a car. Fifth, they know those they teach, not simply as names but in terms of what motivates them, what catches their interest and what turns them off. They also treat those they teach with respect. Finally, these teachers tend to believe in what they do. They see it as worthwhile and as making a difference. At times, their enthusiasm shows and the children benefit from that (Leinhardt and Greeno 1986; Hattie 2004).

But how did they get like that? How did they become so good at their jobs? The essential ingredient has to be a *desire* to be a good teacher, but teaching is very complex and merely wanting to be a good teacher does not make you one. You have to attend to several processes. These include:

- getting to know the children (including knowing what is within their grasp and how they are likely to respond and behave);

- getting to know what has to be taught (including knowing what counts as knowledge, understanding and skills in a particular subject or topic);

- planning (including strategies for scene-setting, eliciting prior knowledge, embedding learning in a meaningful context, fostering understanding, providing instructions for activities, designing simple routines); and

- monitoring learning and acting on it (including using it in planning and when providing feedback to support learning (see, for instance, Rosenshine and Stevens (1986) and Newton (2000)).

## Getting to know the children

Each year will bring you a unique class. A lesson that went well one year could be a flop in the next. No-one can tell you precisely how each child will respond to your lessons but you can, at least, start with some useful generalisations about children. You can use these as a skeleton and add flesh as you learn more about the particular children in front of you.

Children in the primary school, of course, are growing. Bones become longer and grow harder. Those of the skull, hands and feet harden before the others. With a parallel development in muscles and muscle control, greater manipulative skills are possible. What is physically possible for them changes every year. For example, six-year-olds may be able to kick a ball and run after it. Only later will they be able to run with the ball at their feet.

### Case study 4.1

#### A head above the rest

John was always tall for his age and stood a head taller than the others in the class. Teachers saw him as inattentive and blamed any deficiencies in his progress on that. His parents had been told of this and they added their disapproval to the teacher's. In reality, John was no more inattentive than the rest. It was simply that his inattention was noticed more. Deficiencies in his progress probably had another cause, as yet unidentified.

## Activity 4.1

Observe a Key Stage 1 child and a Key Stage 2 child. What can the older child do as a result of greater physical development that the younger child cannot do or, at best, can do only imperfectly? How might the differences affect learning opportunities?

Even if children came equipped with fully developed muscles and bones, they would still not perform like adults. This, of course, is because the brain does not come fully developed. Jean Piaget's description of children's intellectual development is probably the best known account of how the intellect unfolds. He identified stages that are particularly relevant to your work: a pre-operational stage (spanning about 2 to 7 years), a concrete operations stage (about 7 to 12 years) and a formal operations stage (post-11 years).

Children begin to use symbols early in the pre-operational stage. For example, they use one thing to represent another, like a brush used as a horse. During this period, children begin to sort and classify things in simple ways (such as brown and white loaves) but tend to focus on only one division at a time. Sorting loaves of bread into brown and white is possible but sorting them into brown and white, sliced and uncut, is unlikely. They tend to see the world only from their own point of view. What it looks like to them is the way it looks to everyone. They tend to think a number of sweets that are spread out amount to more sweets than the same number in a compact group. They may say that a curled up piece of string is shorter than an identical piece that is straight. They are also likely to say there is more water in a tall, narrow glass than in a short, stubby one of greater volume and that there is more clay in a sausage shape than when it is rolled into a ball.

In the middle years (the concrete operations stage) children do recognise that spreading out sweets does not make more of them, that curling up a string does not make it shorter, that the shape of the vessel does not affect the quantity of water in it, and that rolling out a piece of clay does not increase its volume. Perhaps more importantly, they become quite good at making generalisations from what they see around them. For example, they see that balls bounce, and so come to expect all balls to bounce. One that does not bounce attracts a lot of attention. Similarly, they find that hollow things float in the bath, and so believe that all hollow things float. This is a very powerful ability, but limited experience can lead them astray – not all hollow things float. On the other hand, the children's ability to use deductive reasoning chains is not strong at this stage. Although they may play at being Sherlock Holmes, in practice they are unlikely to be good detectives until the end of the stage. At that point they can reason about problems of this kind: John is taller than Jane and Jane is taller than Fred; is John taller than Fred? But to present long, deductive arguments before this time is likely to be counter-productive. Children are still learning to handle and manipulate information in working memory and the mechanics which help them may still be developing (Demetriou *et al.* 2002). It may be this developing capacity to handle information that gives rise to the intellectual stages we observe. Your approach will take advantage of the way the child thinks and will reflect the child's stage of intellectual development.

## Case study 4.2

### Managing thinking

Joe's class was practising mental arithmetic. This can draw heavily on the ability to handle figures in working memory. After some easy questions, he asked for the answer to $4 \times 99$. They gasped and complained that it was too hard to do in their heads.

'Oh, do you think so? Let me try – $4 \times 99$, hmm! that is hard. Let's see – 99 is nearly 100. Four $\times$ 100; that's easy. It's 400. But that's too much. I wonder by how much. Each hundred is one more than 99. We did four hundreds so that is 4 more. If I take those four off, then it'll be right; 400 with four off is . . .'

'396', the children responded.

'So $4 \times 99$ is 396', Joe concluded. The children tried it on paper and confirmed the answer.

'Try this one: $3 \times 99$', said Joe. He talked the children through it, then asked them the answers to $5 \times 99$, $5 \times 20$, $5 \times 19$, $5 \times 29$, $5 \times 20$ again, $5 \times 21$, $5 \times 101$, $5 \times 98$, and so on. After each one, he talked the procedure through.

This illustrates Joe developing a specific thinking skill in mental arithmetic. This one reduces the burden on working memory and makes it possible for the children to do more with the available space. (For an introduction to helping children think in effective ways see Higgins (2001). For a discussion of the concepts and debates involved in teaching thinking skills see Smith (2002).)

## Activity 4.2

Ask the class teacher about other examples of specific thinking skills that he or she tries to develop in the children. Can you construct another useful specific thinking skill yourself for your specialist subject area?

But while we have the potential for reason, we are also emotional creatures. By school age, children can show a wide range of emotions, including joy, fear, anger, embarrassment, shame and guilt. They have usually developed some emotional self-control and can generally interact with others, but not always successfully. Some variation stems from parenting patterns. For instance, the children of permissive parents are more likely to lack self-control. Those of authoritarian parents can be subdued and lack social competence. Parents of children from different cultures may press for different skills at different ages. At the same time, children within a family can differ in their moods and responses. Some have a cheerful disposition while others seem to be in a perpetual despond. Emotions can predispose us to think and behave in certain ways. For instance, we know what makes us feel good, and we tend to persist with activities that make us feel good. Embarrassment, on the other hand, can have the opposite effect. What makes children feel good or embarrasses them depends on the culture the children are in. As a general rule, what threatens a child's self-concept or the image the child wants to convey is likely to arouse negative responses. (This is not to say the self-concept or preferred image is always appropriate, as in the case of a bully.) Table 4.1 illustrates some of the effects of emotions on motivation and learning. At times, such effects can be obvious but often they are subtle and can pass unnoticed.

## Some examples of emotions and their effects

Although each emotion is given in a subject context, it could occur in any activity.

The body is what the mind has to work with. As a tool for interacting with the external world, it grows and is capable of more as time passes. At the same time, the mind becomes more adept at using it. Nevertheless, you should not think of the body as a mere appendage of the mind. The two interact so that what goes on in the mind is, in part, shaped by the body. Remember, too, that while we are potentially rational beings, we are not always *primarily* rational beings and emotions play a large part in shaping what we think, learn and do.

When it comes to self-controlled behaviour, very young children tend to follow rules, whatever they are, if they are backed by some kind of punishment. By school age, children see a rule as justified if it suits them. Only later do children see moral action as living up to the expectation of others and 'being good' as important for its own sake.

### Case study 4.3a

#### Good today and bad tomorrow

One child in a nursery school was so well behaved one day that she was awarded a Smiley Face badge. The next day, she was quarrelsome and unco-operative. When her mother asked her about the change, she said, 'I used up all my good, yesterday'.

### Activity 4.3

Speculate on other reasons for her behaviour. How would you respond?

**TABLE 4.1**   Examples of emotions and their effects

| | |
|---|---|
| **Embarrassment** | The teacher introduces a new topic in Mathematics. She says, 'This is easy! You'll all be able to do this!' A child fails to understand. Emotion: embarrassment, reducing motivation and increasing a belief that she has not got what it takes in maths. |
| **Sadness** | In English, the teacher reads a story about an animal whose grandpa dies. Emotions: sadness, empathy. Through identifying with the animal, the children learn to recognise and cope with this emotion. |
| **Feeling curious** | The teacher introduces a Feely Box in Science. The children are keen to test their sense of touch to identify the contents. Emotions: associated with curiosity and the hope to show competence, feelings of developing self-efficacy and positive motivation for next lesson. |
| **Shame** | In History, the talk is of the way the poor lived in 'olden times'. One child feels that his much-loved grandpa's way of life is being disparaged. Emotions: the child feels shame (but does not show it) and argues aggressively in defence of harsher ways of life. |
| **Anxiety** | In Geography, the teacher sets the children a number of tasks. Emotion: one child is inclined to be anxious. She sees others making faster progress so rushes her work to catch up. |
| **Anger** | The teacher presents a moral dilemma in RE. The children take sides and the debate becomes heated. Emotions: rising anger and defensiveness on both sides in an attempt to avoid being the ones to lose face. |
| **Moods** | In teaching a new skill in PE, the teacher is positive about progress. Emotions: those with happy dispositions improve; those with sad dispositions show no change. When the teacher is negative about progress, the happy ones do not change and the sad ones improve. |
| **Fear** | The teacher brow-beat and intimidated the children in many lessons. Emotion: the children were generally fearful and endeavoured to avoid being noticed. They gave little attention to the lessons but could recall in detail the teacher's anger over a minor matter and were indignant at the injustice of it. |
| **Depression** | Children often measure themselves against others by checking how others are doing. One whispers to another in a mathematics lesson, 'What number are you on?' The other child scoffs at the first for being so far behind and draws the attention of neighbours to it. Emotion: depression, shame and consequent demotivation in these lessons until the teacher sets about raising the child's self-esteem and self-efficacy. |

**Case study 4.3b**

A slightly older girl hit one of the boys in the playground. When the teacher asked her why, she said: 'Because he wouldn't play with me'.

'Did he play with you after you hit him?' asked the teacher.

'No!' replied the child.

'So, if he won't play with you tomorrow, will you hit him again?'

'Yes!' insisted the child.

This teacher was trying to bring the child to connect her behaviour with its consequences with the intention of bringing her to see the need for self-control. What would you say next?

**Activity 4.4**

Focus on a child interacting with others. Why does the child interact? What does the child get out of it? Do emotions play a part? Does intellect (thinking) play a part? How do these relate to one another in the interaction you observed?

Given the variation in genetic make-up and the very different worlds we can grow up in, you will not be surprised that there can be wide variations between children. Perhaps the surprise ought to be more the extent to which children are the same. For instance, in spite of the differences, children develop physically in similar ways and the order in which they go through Piaget's stages is the same. Development is not, however, entirely rigid, and some children may move through a stage faster than others. Even a child who is in a particular stage may not be irrevocably locked in it, particularly when the context is very familiar to the child and the language used is familiar. Habits and fixed patterns of behaviour develop from an early age. Within a given stage of intellectual development, children may develop preferred ways of thinking and learning and much has been written about matching your teaching style to their individual learning styles. How effective this is is uncertain (Klein 2003). In any case, it may be more useful for children in the primary school to experience and learn to handle a range of teaching and learning styles. So, while you must recognise that the children operate at, say, the concrete level, you could present information in a variety of ways using, for example, words, pictures and real objects, and help them construct understandings through a mix of discussion, gesture, direct experience, and whole-class, group and independent activity.

## Getting to know what has to be taught

At a glance, this seems a straightforward task. Getting to know what you will have to teach cannot be a difficult task. After all, you are not preparing the children for their finals at university. The content you see in school books for children is fairly straightforward and, for an adult, relatively undemanding. But, as with most things, there is a little more to it than that (Shulman 1986; Grossman 1990; Calderhead 1996).

First, there is knowing the subject. It is often said that you never really know a subject until you have to teach it. Teaching makes you put your knowledge in order, relate the parts and fit in all those confusing bits. In other words, you have to understand it yourself. New teachers spend a lot of time doing this and simplifying the ideas so they are meaningful to the children. Expert teachers have done this and know the key themes and ideas and what the subject is about. They know that subjects are not collections of facts and figures to be learned, and their understanding allows them to ask 'Why?' questions and press the children to think about their answers. Other teachers may, sometimes without knowing it, see a subject simply as facts to be acquired (a view that is reinforced by some kinds of attainment tests). They drill the children so they can recall this information on demand. At the end of a lesson, the teacher and the children probably feel very satisfied with what they have achieved but it is less than what the expert does. Their children see the subject as offering an understanding of the world and a way of finding out about it, as well as a collection of facts (Newton 2000; Newton and Newton 2000).

Second, there is knowing the analogies, examples, explanations, anecdotes, demonstrations and activities you might use to help children understand the content. It also helps a lot if you know how the children already think about that content. For instance, in science children often think that if you blow up a balloon with air and release it, it will float to the ceiling. Such views (also known as misconceptions or alternative conceptions) have been acquired through direct but limited experience and can be quite resistant to change. A common strategy is to bring out such ideas by discussion and, if possible, confront them with contradictory experience. In this case, you could blow up some balloons, fasten and release them, so the children observe them fall to the floor.

Third, there is knowing the materials and resources, how you might use them and how you might put things into a sequence so that learning is progressive. Words are cheap and it is the materials and resources that often shape what you and the children can do. This begins with pencils, paper and books and extends to apparatus and tools. For instance, in PE, what you can do is limited without a safety mat and, with one, a vaulting box adds to the possibilities. Then you must think about the learning sequence you will aim for, not in the abstract, but with the real objects in front of you.

## Case study 4.4

### The bare bones of a lesson plan

Vicky's science lesson was about the human skeleton. She remembered general points about the skeleton from her own school days, especially a set of useful analogies (the skull is like a crash helmet that protects the brain, the ribs make a cage around the heart and lungs, and the arm and leg bones are like hollow tubes with ball and hinge joints). The children's science book reminded her of some relevant details and made the important point that our skeletons give us shape. She knew that the children would not really grasp the import of this without help, but what could she do? The thought of not having a shape brought Mr Blobby to mind. Vicky found a dustbin bag and put in a few internal 'organs' (a ball, two balloons and a length of rope. Mr Blobby, of course, subsided into a shapeless heap on the table. She now put a long-legged stool inside. This gave him shape so he no longer subsided in a heap. Next, she went to the science cupboard where she found a small, plastic skeleton, an animal's skull and a wallchart showing the bones of the human skeleton.

She felt she now had sufficient subject knowledge (details of the skeleton and its function), pedagogical knowledge (analogies) and resources (the Mr Blobby model, the model skeleton and wallchart) to plan a lesson. In practice, these three kinds of knowledge would probably be closely connected so that recalling one brings the others into mind (Newton 2004).

## Activity 4.5

Look at a Key Stage 2 textbook for a subject that is very different to your own specialism. Do you see anything that you did not know? If yes, how will you overcome this when planning a lesson?

## Planning teaching

When you watch expert teachers, they make it look effortless. It may even seem that they achieve this without planning but they carry a lot of the detail in their heads. They have tried, adjusted and refined approaches over several years so that much of what they do needs no script or aide-memoire. But do not let that fool you; there *is* a plan and these experts work through it and, when the need arises, deviate from it to achieve their goals.

Goals are what you should begin with. If you do not know where you are going, how will you know when you have got there? You need to be very clear about your goals, aims or targets at the outset. Your content knowledge will guide you with these but be as specific as possible. Ask yourself, 'What do I want the children to know, understand and be able to do at the end of the lesson?' Keep your goal list short and, once you have it, keep referring to it as you plan how you will achieve the goals.

Give some thought to how you will set the scene. This is to help turn the children's minds to the topic in hand and it brings relevant knowledge into conscious thought. Explore this knowledge with questions and look for misconceptions. Extend the children's knowledge, if necessary, to suit the topic in hand. When you introduce the topic, give it a meaningful context. Perhaps embed it in a story or some familiar event. All this preparation will help the children relate new knowledge to their existing knowledge. Knowledge that is tied together in this way is more durable than isolated fragments.

Understanding is about noticing relationships. When you explain, keep the steps small and fill in the knowledge gaps so that the children do not become lost as they listen. Draw their attention to the relationships. Use conceptual models to highlight them. For example, a picture of an owl hovering over half a dozen mice which are placed above fifty ears of wheat is a graphic model of a food pyramid. Its shape reflects the relationship. Analogies can help children understand complex or invisible processes but be sure that the children know the basis of your analogy well. For instance, they are probably very familiar with an orange, so an orange might be used to represent the Earth with the peel being like the Earth's crust. Show a real orange next to a globe of the Earth to make the analogy more immediate, compelling and memorable. But take care that the children know the limits of an analogy. You would not want them to think that the Earth had seeds inside it.

If the children listen passively, they may not bother to make mental connections. Make them active listeners by focusing questions on the connections. Have them make predictions. This makes them relate their items of information in order to provide you with an answer. Press them to explain in their own words, translate information into another form (for example, making words into a picture), think of another example, and apply what they have just acquired. Bear in mind the intellectual stage of the children and make things as concrete as you can. Give them lots of hand-on activities to think with so that they can construct understandings themselves. Explore those understandings with the children and help them extend them through talk, use and activity (Newton 2000, 2001).

## Case study 4.5

### Routines

Simon used the first Design and Technology lesson of the year to introduce some routines. He reminded the children that they all knew who he was but he was awful at remembering names. He asked what they could do to help him. It was agreed that they would design and make name badges. Several kinds of badges were passed around and examined. Simon told the children what he meant by designing. He had some of them relate in their own words what he meant. Paper and pencils for designing, and materials and card snips for making, were in trays for each pair of children and were neatly stacked on a side table. Simon told the children that one person from each pair was to join an orderly queue at the side table. When he was satisfied with the queue, he allowed them to take a tray. At the end of the lesson, the other member of the pair returned the tray to the table and stacked it neatly. This queuing routine was one that Simon insisted on whenever there were things to be distributed, whatever the lesson. The children soon learned what was expected and knew that if they were disorderly, the teacher would make them do it all again, delaying the start of activities which they generally liked.

## Activity 4.6

Over a complete lesson, note the routines a teacher uses to maintain:

(a) order;

(b) effective working; and

(c) considerate interactions.

Your class do not return materials to their correct places after use. Devise a simple routine to eliminate the problem.

Routines allow events to run smoothly, particularly during changeover times. For example, Simon always began the day in the same way by calling the children to order and insisting on silence while he checked the register. This helped to settle them and clearly marked the beginning of the day's events. He never allowed that mark to become fuzzy by delaying events but went straight into business. At the end of the day, his routine was to bring the children to order and have them tidy the room and their tables. Simon then stood at the door and dismissed the children by tables, taking the opportunity to say a word of praise to some deserving child as he or she left.

Such routines do not happen by themselves. They are planned and practised until they become almost self-running. However, keep them simple or you will not maintain them (Newton 2005).

## Monitoring learning and acting on it

You need to monitor the children's learning so you can gauge the effectiveness of your teaching, and tell the children how to do better. Ideally, you need to know things are going wrong as soon as that happens so that you can remedy matters before you have a big problem. This means you should monitor learning as you talk, explain, discuss, demonstrate or otherwise interact with the children. You do it by asking them, for example, to recall things, explain them in their own words, translate words into a picture, provide an example, make a prediction, and apply their new learning. While the responses give you clues about the quality of the learning, there is a bonus. All this questioning reduces the opportunity for children to be passive learners, it engages them with the topic and can add to your press for understanding. For instance, you can press children to elaborate on responses by explaining their answers.

When you respond to their answers, you are generally advised to be moderate in your praise so that you do not devalue the currency. 'That's right!' is often praise in itself. If you sometimes respond with 'That's a good answer because . . .', it can let the others know the kind of answer they should construct. If you find that the children have not understood, talking on is pointless. You will have to backtrack and locate where their understanding broke down and have another try or try another approach.

## Case study 4.6

### Supporting understanding

The teacher wanted the children to understand the need to care for the environment. She had a large, stuffed, toy seal on her lap and began by asking children what it was, where it lived and what it ate. The seal 'told' the story of her happy life in the sea until one day a ship sailed past and spilled oil everywhere. At this point, the teacher checked that the children knew what oil was. She went on to tell the children that the seal's eyes became sore and swollen so she could not see. Here, the teacher asked the children if they had ever had sore eyes and what it was like. For days, she swam around not knowing where she was. She became thinner and thinner because she could not catch any fish to eat. She almost died but some people rescued her just in time and helped her to get well again.

The teacher checked the children's grasp of the story and asked for their opinions about what the ship did. She did not stop there but introduced another instance for the children to talk about. The painters had spilled some paint on the school field. The children knew of this because they had been warned to keep away from it.

T: 'Do you think it matters? Is spilled paint on the grass a good thing or a bad thing or does it not matter?

C1: 'The grass might die.'

C2: 'Worms and things underneath might die.'

C3: 'Birds might die.'

T: 'Why might they die?'

C3: 'The grass can't grow with paint on it and then there's nothing for the worms and things to eat.'

The teacher took this as evidence that these young children had grasped the central message of the lesson (Newton 2002).

## Activity 4.7

Observe a teacher introducing and developing a topic. How does the teacher support:

(a) the learning of facts (knowing what); and

(b) understanding (knowing why)?

How do the two differ?

You do not, of course, stand in front of the class and talk all the time. Often, you have the children engage in tasks or practical activities. This does not mean that monitoring stops and you watch the grass grow. You now have the chance to monitor each child's learning on a one-to-one basis. Go from child to child and ask about the activity, pressing them to, for instance, explain why they are doing things in a particular way. Toward the end of the session, however, you will often bring the children together and review the topic. This is your chance to check that their learning hangs together in a coherent way.

Finally, the children's written responses to tasks you have set provide you with another opportunity to gauge each child's learning. Check the work promptly. Anything you have to say loses its value if it comes weeks after the work was done. As well as checking the work, provide advice which tells the child clearly and in simple terms how to improve. If necessary, exemplify it. Take time over how you evaluate the work. If you say a piece of work is bad, some children will take this to mean they have not got what it takes to do any better. Since they do not have what Hercule Poirot calls his 'little grey cells', why bother? You need to show that you believe they have what it takes and what is needed is effort and time on their part. What is more, you expect them to show it to be true. High expectations often harm no-one and can do some good, particularly if you help the child learn the value of persistence (Rosenshine and Stevens 1986; Newton 2002).

## Be a creative teacher

It would be a rare teacher who was an expert at the outset; becoming an expert takes time. But some people teach for 40 years and those years are all the same. Others teach for 40 years and have 40 different years. Aim to improve your teaching skills each year. Think about what did and did not work and use it to plan something new and better. Creativity is not something you foster only in the children. Keep it alive in yourself and, if you do, you will always find some satisfaction in your teaching, even on the day you retire.

## Activity 4.8

Would you describe yourself as enthusiastic? Rate yourself on a 0–5 point scale.

Do you consider yourself to be creative? Rate yourself similarly.

Observe enthusiasm expressed by a teacher who is teaching something he or she enjoys. How do the children respond?

How does a teacher's creativity in constructing and delivering lessons show itself?

How does this affect the teacher's behaviour?

## Conclusion

Teaching is a bit like driving a car. Some drive it well and some drive it badly. It helps if you know what the car can do, cannot do and might do if conditions are right. It also helps if you know what good driving looks like and what you might do to help you become a good driver. And, like changing gear, much of what you do can become automatic. When that happens, you don't have to think about the detail, you just do it. This gives you space to think several steps ahead and orchestrate your teaching so that the quality of learning is better. Of course, like any analogy, it has its limits. For instance, you may come to understand the children in your class but not, I hope, in the same way that you understand your car. Teaching involves more and needs more subtlety than driving a car. At the same time, although practice makes skills automatic, you must remember that automatic responses can also make you resistant to change (Borko and Putnam 1996). Over your teaching career, expectations and approaches will change so you may need to develop new habits and ways of working in the future.

In this chapter, I have listed some of the things an expert teacher attends to. But there are other things that shape what happens in the classroom. Some event beyond the school walls, for instance, can make even an expert teacher's efforts fail. No-one can be ready for every eventuality or has perfect lessons all the time. What you aim to do is improve so that your good lessons predominate and overwhelm those few bad moments we all experience from time to time in teaching.

## Suggestions for further reading

If you would like to explore some of the issues touched upon in this chapter, the following books should be of interest to you:

Higgins, S.E. (2001) *Thinking through Primary Teaching*. Cambridge: Chris Kington Publishing.

This book provides an introduction to work on thinking skills and their place in the primary classroom, including a useful range of ideas and activities for teachers to use.

Newton, D.P. (2000) *Teaching for Understanding*. London: RoutledgeFalmer.

The subtitle of this book, *What It Is and How to Do It*, encapsulates the essence of the book. The theoretical underpinnings of teaching for understanding are discussed and then related to a range of contexts and examples to illustrate how teachers can translate theory into practice.

## References

Borko, H. and Putnam, R.T. (1996) 'Learning to teach', in D.C. Berliner and R.C. Calfee (eds) *Handbook of Educational Psychology*. New York: Macmillan, pp. 673–705.

Calderhead, J. (1996) 'Teachers: beliefs and knowledge', in D.C. Berliner and R.C. Calfee (eds) *Handbook of Educational Psychology*. New York: Macmillan, pp. 709–25.

Demetriou, A., Christou, C., Spanoudis, G. and Platsidou, M. (2002) *The Development of Mental Processing: Efficiency, Working Memory and Thinking*. Monographs of the Society for Research in Child Development. Boston, MA: Blackwell.

Grossman, P. (1990) *The Making of a Teacher*. New York: Teachers College Press.

Hattie, J. (2004) 'The expert vs. the experienced teacher'. Seminar, July, University of Newcastle upon Tyne.

Higgins, S.E. (2001) *Thinking through Primary Teaching*. Cambridge: Chris Kington Publishing.

Klein, P.D. (2003) 'Rethinking the multiplicity of cognitive resources and curricular representations: alternatives to learning styles and multiple intelligences'. *Journal of Curriculum Studies*, **35**, 45–81.

Leinhardt, G. and Greeno, J.G. (1986) 'The cognitive skills of teaching'. *Journal of Educational Psychology*, **78**, 75–95.

Moallem, M. (1998) 'An expert teacher's thinking and teaching and instructional design models and principles: an ethnographic study'. *Education, Training, Research and Development*, **46**, 37–64.

Newton, D.P. (2000) *Teaching for Understanding*. London: RoutledgeFalmer.

Newton, D.P. (2001) 'Helping children understand'. *Evaluation & Research in Education*, **15**, 119–27.

Newton, D.P. (2002) *Talking Sense in Science*. London: RoutledgeFalmer.

Newton, D.P. (2004) *Teaching Tricky Science Concepts*. Leamington Spa: Scholastic.

Newton, D.P. (2005) *Teaching Design and Technology, 3–11*, London: Sage.

Newton, D.P. and Newton, L.D. (2000) 'Do teachers support causal understanding through their discourse when teaching primary science?' *British Educational Research Journal*, **26**, 599–613.

Rosenshine, B. and Stevens, R. (1986) 'Teaching functions', in M.C. Wittrock (ed.) *Handbook of Research on Teaching*. New York: Macmillan, pp. 376–91.

Schulman, L.S. (1986) 'Paradigms and research programs in the study of teaching', in M.C. Wittrock (ed.) *Handbook of Research on Teaching*. New York: Macmillan, pp. 3–36.

Smith, G.F. (2002) 'Thinking skills: the question of generality'. *Journal of Curriculum Studies*, **34**, 659–78.

# Planning for teaching and learning

## Eve English

## Introduction

Planning and assessment are at the heart of effective teaching. They are dealt with in separate chapters in this book but each must inform the other. The Qualified Teacher Status (QTS) Standards (TTA 2002) for planning are far-reaching but necessary both in terms of supporting your teaching and ensuring the successful learning of your pupils.

Although experienced teachers are increasingly being asked to complete more detailed teaching plans these will still not be as comprehensive as the ones that you will compile and there is, of course, a very good reason for this. You need to have thought through every aspect of your lesson from that very important learning objective to the resources needed, the organisation of your teaching, the differentiation for individual pupils, the pace of the lesson and even the questions you are going to ask the children. Before we get on to that level of detail, however, we are going to consider the 'whole picture', the way your lesson planning fits into the way the school has organised general planning and the planning of each curricular area to ensure continuity and progression and breadth and balance, for example.

## Long-term planning

In most schools long-term planning will be in place when you go into school. Typically, there will be a policy document that sets out the general requirements for school planning.

The following case study is an example of a junior school's long-term general curriculum policy that will inform planning for individual curriculum areas.

Long-term planning for each subject area will be based on the general curriculum document and will be drawn up by the staff, led by the co-ordinator of each subject.

## Case study 5.1

*General Curriculum Policy*

### Role of teachers

Teachers are expected to:

- Provide a challenging and stimulating curriculum designed to enable all children to reach the highest standards of personal achievement;
- Recognise and be constantly aware of the needs of each individual child according to ability and aptitude;
- Ensure that all teaching addresses progression and continuity;
- Maintain an up-to-date knowledge of National Curriculum programmes of study, and allow all children access to the National Curriculum regardless of gender or race;
- Work collaboratively with a shared philosophy and commonality of practice.

Support staff are encouraged to work on raising pupils' understanding of what is required of them and how to achieve it rather than simply rehearsing or doing tasks for children.

### Role of the co-ordinator

Co-ordinators are expected to:

- Take the lead in policy development and the production of schemes of work designed to ensure progression and continuity throughout the school;
- Support colleagues in their development of detailed work plans and implementation of the scheme of work and in assessment and record-keeping activities;
- Monitor progress and advise the head teacher on action needed;
- Take responsibility for the purchase and organisation of central resources;
- Keep up to date with developments in designated subject areas and disseminate information to colleagues as appropriate.

### Equal opportunities

The school is committed to working towards equality of opportunity in all aspects of school life. Our aim is to offer all our pupils a curriculum that is relevant and differentiated so that all our pupils may reach their full potential and grow in self-esteem. It is of great importance to ensure equal access to the curriculum and equal status for all learners. Teachers must ask themselves whether the curriculum has met the needs of all pupils.

### Planning

Planning is a process in which all teachers are involved. Policy documents and curriculum guidelines are developed by curriculum co-ordinators in collaboration with the whole staff. Termly plans and clearly identified learning objectives are written by individual teachers and monitored by the head teacher. Regular staff meetings are used to discuss various aspects of the curriculum and to ensure consistency in approach and standards.

## Teaching and learning

Teaching and learning are at the heart of school life. It is the means by which we offer, and put into practice, a curriculum that is broad and balanced and meets the requirements of the National Curriculum, religious education and collective worship.

Our purposes and aims for teaching and learning are that all children will:

- Achieve their full potential in terms of academic progress, aesthetic appreciation and spiritual awareness;
- Be tolerant, sensitive and understanding, showing respect for the rights, views and property of others;
- Develop a responsible and independent attitude towards their work and towards their role in society.

## Strategies for teaching and learning

A variety of modes of working are utilised – group work, paired or individual tasks and whole-class teaching, where appropriate. Groups are normally of mixed ability, although matched ability groups are used for particular purposes. Relevant discussion and interactive, collaborative learning is encouraged, although there are times of the day set aside for quiet, individual tasks. The emphasis of our teaching and learning policy is on first-hand experience and we encourage children to participate freely in investigational work, to communicate findings in a variety of ways and to become actively involved in decision-making.

It is up to the teacher's professional judgement as to how the curriculum should be delivered in the classroom. Teaching styles and classes vary, and what is appropriate in one situation may not necessarily work in another. Whenever possible, studies should be enquiry-based and teachers should enable this to happen.

## Assessment

The assessment of pupils' work is covered by our Assessment Policy. However, it is very important that assessment is linked to planning. Formative assessment is used to guide each child's progress in each aspect of the subject, determining what each child has learned and what, therefore, should be the next stage in his/her learning.

## Organisation

The curriculum is organised as part of an integrated approach to learning whereby:

- It is sometimes necessary to teach skills separately before they are used in topic work or to ensure progression throughout the curriculum;

- Lessons can involve whole-class teaching, co-operative group work or individual work as appropriate.

- There is no specialist teaching; subjects are taught by all class teachers;

- Pupils with special educational needs are able to develop confidence and express their feelings;

- The emphasis in our teaching is on practical experience and we encourage children to take control of their own learning;

- Excellence is celebrated through display and performance;

- Pupils are encouraged to take responsibility for care and storage of resources.

## Cross-curricular links

Subjects are mainly taught separately but every effort is made to show links with other areas of the curriculum. We try to identify cross-curricular opportunities at the planning stage. We also draw children's attention to the links so that they can see that subjects are not isolated.

## Working with parents

The school is committed to working with parents and recognises the vital role they have in helping children develop in all curriculum areas.

## Staff training

All members of staff have the opportunity to attend LEA courses and in-service training (INSET) organised by other agencies. Relevant information is disseminated to other staff members through INSET days and staff meetings. Members of staff are encouraged to attend courses, review resources, mount exhibitions, liaise with our feeder infant and secondary schools and update them-selves on information and approaches to all curriculum areas in order to help improve and monitor teaching. Staff INSET will be organised when appropriate.

## Resources

Each classroom is equipped with a collection of basic resources for each area of the curriculum. These resources are the responsibility of the class teacher. All resources should be appropriate, accessible and clearly labelled. Children are made aware of where resources are kept and the rules for their access and use. Children are encouraged to act independently on choosing, collecting and returning resources where appropriate. Teachers and children work together to establish an attractive, welcoming and well-organised environment.

Central resources are generally the responsibility of the curriculum co-ordinators, each of whom has a budget for the year. The school uses a variety of published materials to facilitate the teaching of the curriculum but recognises the need for teaching to be 'scheme assisted' not 'scheme driven'. Materials are constantly updated, as new and relevant items become available.

Typically, the planning will:

- address statutory requirements in terms of the National Curriculum;
- reflect recommended curricula such as the National Literacy Strategy (NLS), the National Numeracy Strategy (NNS) or QCA documents for other curriculum subjects;
- ensure that the curriculum is broad and balanced;
- ensure continuity and progression; and
- address issues of equal opportunity.

As a trainee teacher you will need to make yourself aware of the requirements of long-term planning and ensure that it is reflected in your medium- and short-term planning. Although it is not expected that you become involved in long-term planning if the school is involved in changing some aspect of this while you are on placement, it would be a good opportunity to observe the process.

## Medium-term planning

Once the long-term planning is in place, class teachers can consider the next level of planning. Medium-term planning is usually drawn up by the class teacher or teachers of a particular class or year group. You will be required to compile medium-term plans for the class of children you are going to teach. However, you will find that, increasingly in schools, medium-term planning will have been completed by teachers and your job will be to negotiate the lessons that you are going to teach. Medium-term planning should be separate for each curricular area and should:

- be informed by the school's long-term planning;
- address all the work to be undertaken by an identified group of children over a specified period of time, such as a term or half-term;
- identify the relevant parts of the Programmes of Study and Attainment Targets of the National Curriculum;
- identify resources; and
- identify formal assessment opportunities.

If a school's medium-term policy does not contain this level of detail then you will need to provide it for yourself and for anyone who is assessing you against the standards.

Table 5.1 gives a suggested format for medium-term planning for the teaching of literacy. The suggested format from the NLS Framework (DfEE 1998) has been adapted to include the additional information that you will need as a trainee teacher (i.e. resources and assessment opportunities).

In case study 5.2, E. describes how a school went about the process of producing medium-term planning after the introduction of the Literacy Strategy.

**TABLE 5.1** Medium-term planning for literacy

| Week | Phonics, Spelling and Vocabulary | Grammar and Punctuation | Comprehension and Composition | Texts | Resources | Assessment Opportunities |
|------|----------------------------------|-------------------------|-------------------------------|-------|-----------|--------------------------|
| | Continuous Work | Continuous Work | Continuous Work | | | |
| | Learning objectives and brief details of activities | Learning objectives and brief details of activities | Learning objectives and brief details of activities | | | |
| Week 1 | | | | | | |
| Week 2 | | | | | | |
| Week 3 | | | | | | |
| Week 4 | | | | | | |
| Week 5 | | | | | | |
| Week 6 | | | | | | |
| Week 7 | | | | | | |
| Week 8 | | | | | | |

(Adapted from English and Williamson 2005: 168)

## Case study 5.2

The National Literacy Strategy was being introduced and we had an Ofsted inspection coming up so the planning had to be carried out very quickly. I was the English co-ordinator, soon to become the literacy co-ordinator. I attended all the training offered by the LEA and disseminated that information to my colleagues at school. We were all a bit shell-shocked. We had become used to following and planning from the National Curriculum but had never had to follow such a structured and prescribed programme. While teachers in many schools didn't believe we could have this level of prescription imposed on us as a profession, we had Ofsted looming and didn't dare risk the outcome. The status of the NLS has always been that of 'recommended' rather than statutory documentation but there was a sting that if SAT results were not up to standard and the NLS was not being used then Ofsted would not look kindly on the school. So we pressed on.

Our long-term planning was fine; it addressed the National Curriculum requirements and the NLS followed those. We added a section on classroom organisation: a small paragraph for a huge change.

Then on to medium-term planning. The NLS *Framework for Teaching* (DfEE 1998) gave a suggested format for medium-term planning for literacy and we decided to use that. The teachers in each year group then worked together to see how they could organise the objectives to form an appropriate programme for their pupils. The word- and sentence-level work was planned almost in the exact order suggested by the NLS but we had a bit more flexibility with text-level work. Once we realised that the reading and writing objectives were linked, planning became clearer. We literally 'cut and pasted' the objectives on large pieces of paper on the hall floor. Working within the range of texts recommended was not easy at the beginning of this initiative. Publishers had not yet come up with 'snippets' and lesson plans to address every objective and we spent a lot of time finding and buying new resources to meet the requirements. We decided to include all resources needed in our medium-term planning to make life easier thereafter. This initial planning involved a lot of time but it has served us well. Of course, we also had to plan for the teaching of speaking and listening. We are now looking at introducing a little more 'creativity' into the planning of the curriculum with the introduction of the *National Primary Strategy* and *Speaking, Listening, Learning: Working with Children in Key Stages 1 and 2*.

## Short-term planning

## Activity 5.1

Choose any subject of the curriculum and any learning objective. Detail is not important at this point but think about everything you will need to consider to make the lesson a success for you and the pupils. Make a list of headings that you think should go on a planning sheet to help you teach the lesson effectively.

How does your list compare with the list that follows? Short-term planning for any curriculum subject should:

- evolve directly from medium-term planning;
- address all the work to be undertaken in a particular subject by the pupils in a class or year group over a short period of time;
- describe the activities to be undertaken, which should include:

   **1** prior assessment outcomes that will inform planning;
   **2** main learning objectives;
   **3** how the work addresses the appropriate NC Programme of Study;
   **4** timing (date, time, approximate length of the lesson/activity);
   **5** pace (approximate length of each part of the lesson/activity);
   **6** class organisation (whole-class, group or individual work);
   **7** teacher focus (e.g. the teaching of whole class, groups or individuals);
   **8** opportunities for differentiation; and
   **9** assessment targets.

Points 1 and 9 show how closely planning is linked to assessment for learning, or formative assessment.

Figure 5.1 gives you a format for a short-term lesson plan that can be used for most subjects showing clearly how the planning and assessment cycle works. Figure 5.2 is a lesson plan that is designed to help you plan for a science lesson.

## Planning activities

Once you have identified your learning objectives you need to think about the most appropriate learning activities. You may be interested to know that prior to the introduction of the National Curriculum the description of activities was what a typical school would call planning; learning objectives tended to be addressed incidentally. Now the learning objectives drive planning but selecting appropriately motivating activities is still very important. There are many published schemes that will give you ideas that are directly linked to objectives but these can sometimes be limiting and not relate to your particular class of pupils. You need, for example, to think of the different preferred learning styles of the pupils. It would not be possible, or indeed desirable, to try to address all the different styles of learning in one lesson. Nevertheless, you need to vary your lessons to accommodate as many styles as possible. Some children like to listen, some like a more 'hands on' experience, some like to talk and work in groups and others like to be shown what to do. It is therefore not appropriate to deliver all your lessons from the front of the classroom in a didactic way, but nor is it a good idea to let all of your pupils discover things for themselves with minimal involvement from the teacher.

| Date: | Time: | Class: |
|-------|-------|--------|

Subject:

NC Programmes of Study:

Learning objectives:

Relevant information from prior assessment:

Activity:

Resources:

Differentiation:

Group activities:

Lesson:
Introduction (__minutes):

Key questions:

Development (__minutes):

Key Questions:

Conclusion (__minutes):

Key Questions:

Opportunities for assessment:

Additional activities:

Implications from assessment for future planning:

**FIGURE 5.1**   Lesson plan

Within a lesson there will be different parts. You need to think about how these parts affect the whole. In other words you can provide variety within a lesson but there should also be cohesion. One of the criticisms of the structure of the NLS has been the fragmentation of the Literacy Hour and schools are increasingly trying to make the

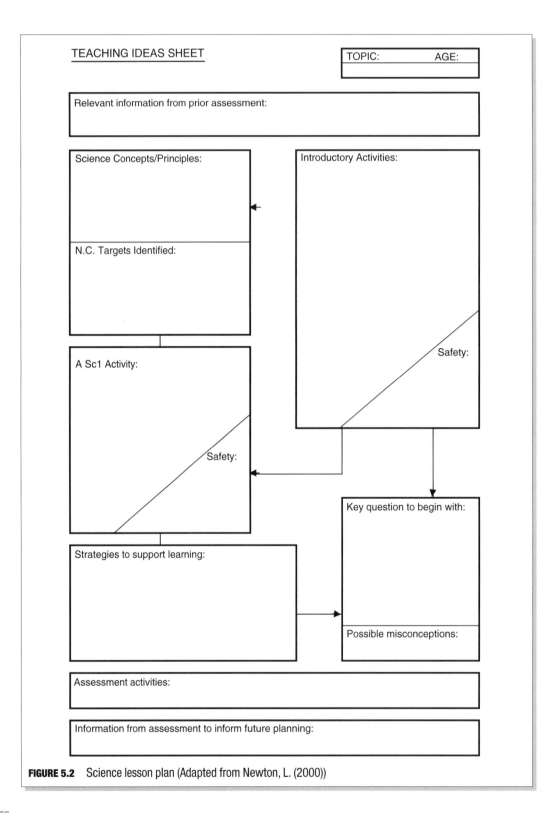

**FIGURE 5.2**   Science lesson plan (Adapted from Newton, L. (2000))

hour more 'joined up' (see case study 1.1 in Chapter 1). The main thing to remember is that the children need to be motivated to engage with the topic and for their learning to develop. You will have to plan carefully and thoughtfully for this.

## Planning resources

From the minute you set foot inside the school in which you are to teach you need to find out what resources are available, where they are kept and how those resources are organised. Think about books, for example. Is there a central library for reference books or are they kept in the classroom? How are 'home reading' books organised? Do you need to organise your preparation around shared resources? Where is all the apparatus for practical science lessons? Where is the photocopier and what are the rules about photocopying? What ICT equipment is available? Will you be using an interactive whiteboard? It is important that your planning lists all the resources you will need to deliver a lesson.

### Activity 5.2

Consider the following Design and Technology activity and *list the resources* that you would need to teach the lesson:

Key Stage 2: Knowledge and understanding of materials and components (DfEE/QCA 1999: 95):
*Pupils should be taught how materials can be combined and mixed to create more useful properties (for example, using cardboard triangles on the corners of a wooden framework to strengthen it).*
The activity is to design and make a land yacht that combines axles and wheels with a framework strengthened with card corners.

The following is a detailed list of resources. How does your list compare?

- 60 cm length of 1 cm square strip wood (Jelutong);
- 30 cm length of dowel for axle;
- A4 card to make card corners;
- piece of card to make the sail;
- glue guns;
- junior hacksaws;
- rule;
- snips (scissors that cut card).

When searching out resources there will always be a host of photocopiable materials available but beware 'death by worksheet'. Remember, children learn in a variety of ways and endless worksheets are not the way to address those different needs or motivate children. Think about the value of group talk, practical lessons, drama, visits beyond the classroom, less obvious writing activities.

## Activity 5.3

In Year 5, term 1 of the NLS, one of the sentence-level learning objectives is 'to revise and extend work on verbs focusing on . . . person: 1st, 2nd and 3rd. Identify and classify examples from reading . . . discuss changes that need to be made and effects on meaning.'

The writing activity that comes at the end of this block of work often involves a worksheet where children are asked to 'translate' a piece of written text from third person to first person. How do you think this writing could be made more meaningful for the children and, therefore, more effective in terms of learning?

One activity could be to get the children to report events as if writing a diary, perhaps writing in role in an historical context, for example. If the children have been fully involved in the drama then they will have a much better understanding of the demands of writing in first person. This activity has asked you to think about the appropriateness of certain resources and, in this particular instance, when not to use them.

## Planning for questioning

It may have struck you as being a little odd that the planning formats suggested above actually asked you to plan the questions that you would ask the children. Is this not too much detail? I would suggest that questioning is very important in terms of effective teaching and learning and that if you can plan the main questions in advance of the lesson then you have a clear idea of how the lesson will progress.

Newton (2002) describes how questioning provides both 'orientation and direction' in a lesson and also helps to monitor a child's thinking:

> When questions are directed towards relationships, causes and effects, and reasons, they en-
> courage the integration of ideas and related facts into the coherent wholes we call under-
> standing. For instance, asking learners for an explanation in their own words is known to
> enhance understanding, presumably because it obliges them to make the mental connections
> needed to construct a response. (*ibid.*: 6)

The aim of your lesson is to ensure that the children have understood what you have intended to teach them and, to this end, the questions you ask are vital. It is, therefore, important that you think about them at the planning stage.

## Planning for differentiation

Each lesson should be planned to address the needs of all pupils. This involves the differentiation of activities. There are many ways in which you can differentiate, including:

■ by outcome – giving the same task to all the pupils but having different expectations;

■ by giving different levels of support;

■ by giving different tasks to suit different needs; and

■ by differentiated questioning.

This last way, the differentiated questioning, is perhaps the most skilful and extremely important when strategies such as the NLS and NNS are requiring more whole-class lessons than was previously the case. Many of these questions will come from the ongoing formative assessment as the lesson progresses but it is well worth thinking about some differentiated questions at the planning stage.

It is important to remember, however, that you cannot possibly have different tasks for all of the 30 children in your class and teachers usually organise the class into three of four ability groups.

## Planning for independent learning

Children only work independently in well-organised classrooms. There will be occasions when children need to get on with tasks without consulting the teacher (e.g. during independent work in the Literacy Hour when the teacher is doing a guided reading/writing activity). This means that the tools the children need must be stored and labelled clearly and be easily accessible. They must know where support materials, such as dictionaries, are kept and they should also know what activities are available to them when their main activity has been completed.

## Conclusion

I hope you have been convinced that detailed planning is essential to teaching effectively. It is certainly one of the areas that NQTs struggle with initially, but remember, you are not being asked to re-invent wheels. Teachers and tutors will support you but the more you are able to put into planning the easier your teaching will be.

## Suggestions for further reading

Newton, L. (2000) 'What do we mean by effective planning of science?', in Newton, L. *Meeting the Standards in Primary Science: A Guide to the ITT NC*. London: Routledge-Falmer.

As well as telling you all you need to know about reflective science teaching the chapter on planning deals with the detail of planning in terms of scientific knowledge and understanding, ensuring progression and continuity.

## References

DfEE/QCA (1999) *The National Curriculum: Handbook for Primary Teachers in England*. London: DfEE.

English, E. and Williamson, J. (2005) *Meeting the Standards in Primary English: A Guide to the ITT NC*. London: RoutledgeFalmer.

Newton, D. (2002) 'Helping children to understand', in Newton, L. (ed.) *Teaching for Understanding Across the Primary Curriculum*. Clevedon: Multilingual Matters.

Newton, L. (2000) *Meeting the Standards in Primary Science: A Guide to the ITT NC*. London: RoutledgeFalmer.

TTA (2002) *Qualifying to Teach: Professional Standards for Qualified Teacher Status and Requirements for Initial Teacher Training*. London: Teacher Training Agency.

# Monitoring and assessing learning

### Helen Cardy

## Introduction

As a trainee teacher you will have started to form your own impression of the meaning and implications of the terms *monitoring* and *assessment* and you will be aware of some of the technical language that accompanies the subject and lends it an air of mystique which can be intimidating. This chapter will help you unpick the mystique of assessment, outline the main types and purposes of assessment, including the statutory requirements, introduce you to methods of assessment and raise your awareness of your own use of assessment in teaching and learning and the implications for your current and future practice.

## The evaluation cycle

Teaching and learning are complex processes which do not fall neatly into sequential or discrete components. However, in order to explain and to understand the teaching and learning process it is necessary to break into these cyclical processes at some point, so we tend to think in broad terms of planning, teaching and assessing. Possibly as a result of this convention, it is common and understandable for those training to teach to view assessment as something which comes at the end of the teaching process, and indeed some trainees, to their cost, choose to 'get to grips' with planning the curriculum and delivering their lessons before they tackle assessment. However, assessment is key to any teaching and learning experience and teaching can only be real teaching if it is related to assessment. In simple terms, if you do not know what you expect learners to be able to do, and you do not know how you will know if and when they can do it, then what is the objective of the lesson and why are you teaching? If you are to be a successful and imaginative teacher who is sensitive to the needs of your pupils it is vital that assessment is an integral part of your teaching and learning from the start. This is not as difficult as it may at first seem because much of what you do as a teacher is monitoring and assessment.

Monitoring and assessment form a continuum of activities which effective teachers do all the time as part of the everyday process of teaching. Every time you ask a meaningful question, have a focused conversation with a child about some writing they have done, mark a piece of work and give the learner feedback; or at the other end of the continuum, when we sit children in a silent room to complete a timed written test and then act upon our findings to move learning on, then we are engaging in some form of assessment. Whenever and however you assess, you are collecting information about what and how children learn and using this information to make judgements and inform planning and future learning experiences. Assessment is about you as a teacher really getting to know about your children and their learning. It is about understanding how best to help them move forward in their learning and about finding keys to help them unlock any misunderstandings. It is an exciting and fascinating aspect of teaching.

## What is assessment?

One definition of assessment is that it is 'the process of gathering, interpreting, recording and using information about learners' responses to an educational task' (Harlen *et al.* 1996).

All assessment involves interpreting learners' responses against expectations which may be either our own expectations as teachers or more formal expectations, often known as standards. As you will be beginning to realise, there are many different types of assessment and each suits a different purpose. Part of the skill in using assessments is to ensure that the right type of assessment is used on a particular occasion and that it is 'fit for purpose'. In order to achieve this you need to know the reason for or purpose of assessing and the range of methods of assessment which are available.

## Where does monitoring fit in?

Monitoring and assessment are often linked together and are closely related. Monitoring is the term used to describe the ongoing process which teachers use to check that everything is as it should be and meets their expectations during a lesson. Most teachers constantly monitor both behaviour and learning. More recently, the term monitoring has been used more specifically to describe the process of checking pupils' progress against their individual targets for learning when tracking their progress. When identifying targets you should ensure they pass the SMART test and be Specific, Measurable, Achievable, Reliable, Relevant and Time-limited. Monitoring is often used to feed into assessment.

# Purposes of assessment

Assessment is often categorised according to its end use and you will need to become familiar with the terminology in order to use the tools of assessment with confidence.

*Formative* assessment includes many of the fairly informal processes which go on continuously in a relaxed and positive atmosphere in the classroom. It provides information to the teacher and the child about the child's preferred learning styles, progress in terms of skills, knowledge and understanding and particular difficulties which individuals or groups may be experiencing. Formative assessment provides teachers and learners with information which helps them to plan future learning, revise teaching and help learners to learn in ways that are appropriate for them. This type of assessment has been found to be influential in raising levels of attainment and therefore the quality of children's learning.

The term *Assessment for Learning* (as opposed to assessment *of* learning) is currently in frequent use to describe this type of assessment but it takes what has passed as formative assessment in the past further by empowering the learner and actively involving them in the assessment process. The Assessment Reform Group (ARG) has used research-based evidence to endeavour to inform and improve assessment for learning and has drawn up principles of assessment for learning (2002) to provide guidance for teachers. The ARG defines assessment for learning as 'the process of seeking and interpreting evidence for use by learners and their teachers to decide where the learners are in their learning, where they need to go and how best to get there'. Realistically, some of this information will be intuitive and much of it will not be written down but will be added to the body of information you hold in your mind about the children you are teaching. However, it is important that you have evidence on which to base your judgements, that you collect this evidence in an informed and structured fashion and that you record it. The evidence needs to go beyond the descriptive to diagnostic if it is to impact on future learning.

*Summative* assessment is the assessment *of* learning. It is used for recording the overall achievement of pupils in a systematic way. It takes place at a specific time and it is a means of communicating the nature and level of achievement to a variety of audiences. Summative assessment can occur at the end of a topic or phase. In primary school, summative assessment takes place at the end of key stages, that is the end of years 2 and 6. There are two basic ways of describing the results of summative assessment and these can affect the way the results are perceived particularly when grades are used. Norm-referenced summative assessment is made against the average performance of a group whereas criterion-referenced assessment is made against a set of criteria, skills or objectives. Theoretically, therefore, everyone can achieve the highest grade in a criterion-referenced summative assessment whereas in a norm-referenced assessment the average or mean score can vary, and it is against this score that others are graded.

You should be aware that there are often problems associated with summative assessment, and while it is often viewed as an objective means of comparing the achievement of a group of learners the assessments themselves can be problematic. If the criteria or standards against which assessment is made are tightly defined then this aids in maintaining consistency across markers, but it also tends to fragment the curriculum by breaking learning down into small, measurable components. However, if the criteria are made more general, they become less reliable as they become dependent on the judgement of individuals as to whether they have been met. It is important that summative assessment is as accurate as possible and 'reliable'. This means that the assessment should produce the same results regardless of when and where it is done, who takes the assessment and who marks the assessment. The test should also be 'fit for purpose' and 'valid'; in other words, it must test what it sets out to test. The scores of some summative assessment are standardised so that they take account, for example, of the differences in ages of children in a particular group, and results can be compared as if the children were the same age. Other factors may be taken into account when standardising scores.

*Diagnostic* assessment is used to find out what a learner already knows, to identify difficulties in learning and to attempt to identify specific learning difficulties in the case of children with special educational needs. For example, diagnostic assessment can be used to identify dyslexia, dyscalculia and similar needs. In the case of diagnostic assessment of children with special educational needs, the assessment is almost always conducted by a professional specialist.

The purpose of *evaluative* assessment is to inform the teacher and the curriculum. As a teacher you can reflect on your teaching and evaluate its effectiveness against various criteria, drawing conclusions and modifying your actions accordingly. When evaluative assessment is published it provides part of the information used in judging the effectiveness of educational institutions. This information is needed to keep the performance of the education system under review but when you are interpreting judgements about school effectiveness it is important to remember that there are many aspects of a school which are not assessed but which, nevertheless, may play an important part in the effectiveness of that school. In evaluative assessment samples may be used rather than assessing all learners. Evaluative assessment is sometimes used when gathering information about a new scheme of work or a new way of delivering the curriculum. Assessment may be against previous performance of learners or a control group of learners who do not follow the programme under evaluation. It is unlikely that you will be in control of this type of assessment as a trainee teacher but its usefulness should not be overlooked.

*Ipsative* (the alternate spelling ipsitive is also acceptable) assessment is used when measuring against the learner's own previous performance. The term 'distance travelled' is sometimes used to describe the amount of improvement demonstrated from a previous assessment of performance or achievement. Ipsative assessment is often used in sport, but may also be used in other subjects. It is known to aid self-esteem and to be motivating for learners because it focuses them on their own learning and improvement and frees them of any tendency to compare themselves with others. Ipsative assessment has been found to be useful in raising boys' achievement. It is a very positive form of assessment.

## The implications of assessment

As with other interactions with children, you need to be particularly sensitive when dealing with issues of assessment. It is important to remember that assessment can and does impact on a child's future. In particular, with summative assessment, achievement is not necessarily a guide to ability. For example, particular types of assessment suit some learners better than others and, unfortunately, no matter how hard we try to make assessment child-friendly, there are those who do not perform well under test conditions or who are simply not in their best health on the day of the assessment. It is always important to consider the impact that assessment may have on self-esteem.

For teachers, assessment impacts upon the curriculum by influencing what is taught and when, and some teachers find themselves under pressure to 'teach to the test', sometimes at the expense of other aspects of the curriculum. The issue of teacher accountability is also made transparent by the results of assessments in that consistent underachievement by pupils in a particular area of the curriculum may indicate a development need of the teacher. Again, there are many factors which can affect the outcome of assessment.

The circumstances of assessment can also affect the outcome for individuals and factors such as age at the time of taking the test, work habits, past achievement and its impact on self-image, the quality of teaching and the relationship between the teacher and the learner, as well as the circumstances at the time of the assessment, including time of day, duration of test, weather and environmental conditions in the assessment room, including temperature, lighting and noise levels, can all affect the result.

## Using monitoring to improve your teaching and learning

Monitoring is a useful technique to develop early in your training because you can use it to inform and improve your teaching. You need to develop observation skills to be aware of what is going on around you, even while focusing your attention on something else, in order to ensure that as many children as possible are benefiting to the maximum from the teaching and learning that is taking place. You will need to use your eyes, your ears and your general awareness (having 'eyes in the back of your head') to ensure behaviour and learning are progressing well. A useful technique is to use your eyes to 'scan' by sweeping them around the room while working with a group. You can gain feedback on your teaching by looking at each pupil and noting their body language and facial expressions as you teach. If things are not going as you wish or you become aware that pupils are becoming restless, or showing signs of disinterest, you need to do some troubleshooting. First, examine the task or the content of your teaching. Do the children understand what you are saying? Is your language and explanation at the right level? Have you been talking for too long? Are the pupils clear about the task they are engaged in and what they are expected to do? Next, examine the organisation of the lesson. Can all the children access the resources they need to complete the task and can they access those resources without disturbing other children? Also, you should examine your groupings. Hopefully, you will have organised your groups in consultation with the children's teacher, but you nevertheless need to be aware of the characters in the class in order to ensure they are organised in such a way as to be capable of collaboration and co-operation.

Monitoring behaviour can present you with some difficulties as you need to monitor both the behaviour of the class in general and of specific individuals. When monitoring the behaviour of the class you need to ensure that all children are on task. Many teachers are particularly sensitive about noise levels and you may find your own views are influenced by those of the head teacher and other colleagues in a particular school. The amount of noise that is acceptable varies according to the task. For example, if children are investigating and debating problems in small groups, then noise often indicates quality learning. If, on the other hand, you are explaining a task, silence would indicate that the children are listening to the instructions. When examining the behaviour of particular children you need to consider how the behaviour you observe compares with their 'norm' and the effect it is having on the learning of others. You then need to consider if, when and how to intervene. You should always intervene when Health and Safety issues are of concern. In monitoring children's responses to questions, always remember to leave them sufficient time to think and self-correct if necessary. Use questions to move their thinking forward. A simple technique is to ask a child why they think as they do and to use a question in answer to children's questions. You should also intervene to clarify a learning point or instructions if your monitoring reveals a misunderstanding.

## Methods of assessment and implications for your practice

It is one thing to know about assessment but you need to know how to go about using assessment effectively in the classroom if you are to meet the Standards for the Award of Qualified Teacher Status and the Induction Standards. It is impossible to tackle all the standards at once, but you should approach your first classroom experience with assessment in mind. Formative assessment does not just happen, and it is important to remember that when preparing for school-based experiences. You should spend some time observing and talking to your mentor about how formative assessment is used to inform short-term planning and how they plan for assessment. Look at planning and note how teachers plan for assessment. Notice how the notes which teachers make on their lesson plans when they evaluate are used and how planning is amended and differentiation is accommodated by the resulting plans.

## Activity 6.1

You have planned a numeracy lesson that addresses the learning objective:
*Read and write numbers to 20* (DfEE/QCA 1999: 63).
As a class teacher, what would you like to know about your pupils' understanding of the lesson? How could you get this information?

You have probably answered the first question by saying that you need to know whether or not the pupils have understood what you have taught. This is *formative* assessment. The process of formative assessment involves gaining a general impression from children's work and language by careful observation and analysis, gradually refining the impression to make a more accurate judgement of the child's aptitude and ability, using your observations to inform your teaching in order to enhance the children's learning and then evaluating the effect of what and how the children have learned following your revisions. When you plan lessons you will need to state your learning objectives and outcomes and you need to plan also the evidence you will use to judge whether the learning outcomes have been met. Activities or products from the lesson need to enable you to make a judgement against your intended objectives. Thus your planning and your assessment are interdependent.

When you are teaching you will be involved in formative assessment when you provide feedback to a child in the form of comments or when you question to elicit responses on which to make judgements. You need to consider key questions at the planning stage, include them in your lesson plans and ensure you use these prepared questions in your lesson, listening carefully to the answers and responding appropriately. Sometimes children will have progressed beyond your learning objectives and this is demonstrated in their responses and questions. When possible, you should try to follow this up with a discussion with the child or group. Asking skilful questions is a key role in teaching. It is important that the range of questions you ask prompts children with supporting comments, probes their understanding during and following teaching, or while the children are engaged in tasks, and assesses the extent to which children can go on to apply what they have learned. You need to make conscious observations of children while you teach them, listening to their comments and discussions and assessing their responses as you teach. Sometimes you will need to make focused observations of particular children, to provide you with additional information or confirm information about their attainment and progress from previous assessments. Observations sometimes need the teacher to be engaged in active discussion with the children about their progress and peer or self-review of their work. This can be usefully carried out in plenaries provided it is relevant to the whole class.

Marking children's work provides an opportunity to provide written feedback. This needs to be positive and motivating, giving guidance and praise when children have met objectives and indicating how and where the work can progress and be improved. Children can and should be involved in analysing and marking their own work.

Short tests can help children immediately with speed of recall and can enable children to see what they have learned and where they need to focus their future attention. Children need to be aware of their targets for learning and be supported in self-assessment of the degree to which they have achieved them. They also need you to diagnose errors with them in order that they can work at correcting them. This is particularly true of recurring errors which may constitute a barrier to progress if not tackled. Some children find this difficult so your support is essential. All of these activities are part of the normal fabric of teaching and learning. You need to keep records as evidence of your formative assessment in order to meet the standards.

## Activity 6.2

As a class teacher what would you need to know about your pupils' level of achievement at the beginning of a school year? What kind of information will the previous class teacher have compiled?

The information you require will be based on *summative* assessment. You will need to engage with summative assessment while you are on school-based experience. These assessments enable schools to provide parents with, and pass on to other teachers, information about pupils' progress as well as providing data which can be used to compare the performance of schools. Some summative assessment is teacher assessment which uses 'attainment targets'. Attainment targets describe the 'knowledge, skills and understanding that pupils of different abilities and maturities are expected to have by the end of each key stage (Curriculum 2000, AT section: 1). At primary level (Key Stage 1 and Key Stage 2) the attainment targets have six level descriptors which describe the type and range of performance that children working at that level may be expected to demonstrate. It is these level descriptors which are used when 'levelling' a piece of work. The process of levelling involves comparing a piece of work with the level descriptors and finding evidence in the work which matches descriptors. This is what is known as a 'best fit' exercise in that you will be matching the work to the level that most closely fits the child's work. It is neither possible nor desirable to work in isolation when levelling as your decisions need to be moderated in order to ensure, as far as possible, that your colleagues would be reaching the same conclusions about particular pieces of work. This can be done by 'blind marking' the work so that your colleagues do not know the grades you have given and then having them 'sample' your marking by selecting a small number of your scripts. This sample can either be random (drawn out of a hat) or you can select a range of work (e.g. two each of lower, middle and higher grades) for your colleagues to cross-mark.

Another method of moderating is to select borderline cases where you are not sure which level to assign, and to seek and make these the targets for cross-marking. If the marks are confirmed you should share your evidence, and if you have given different grades you each need to discuss fully your reasons and the evidence you have selected in assigning a level. Sometimes you may need to involve others, e.g. the subject co-ordinator or the head teacher, in clarifying levels. It is important to annotate work that is to be levelled with the date when the work was done, the amount and nature of support, if any, and any relevant contextual information. If you find you are being consistently too hard or too lenient in your grading, you need to take steps to correct this. Many schools have moderation meetings that involve the whole staff, but if this is not the case in your school you should make sure your work is moderated. While you are training, your class teacher and/or mentor will support you in your assessments. The relative importance and weighting of teacher assessment in making the summative assessments which are formally reported for each child and each school changes with the political and educational climate and, after a period of relative unimportance, teacher assessment is once again beginning to gain more status and, in some cases, replace written, independently marked pencil and paper tests.

You will also need to be involved in Statutory Assessment Tasks (SATs). There is a requirement to complete SATs in English and Mathematics at Key Stage 1 and English, Mathematics and Science at Key Stage 2. In addition, many schools choose to administer optional SATs at the end of each year. These follow a similar format to SATs but are internally marked in schools. They have the advantage of providing tracking data to enable children's progress to be monitored throughout their time at school. They also allow children to become familiar with this more formal assessment procedure. A detailed marking scheme is provided with SATs, together with exemplary material to assist you in making judgements. It is important to remember that SATs only provide a 'snapshot' of attainment and do not, in themselves, provide sufficient information to give a full picture of a learner's achievement.

It is a legal requirement that *Baseline Assessment* is completed in the autumn term in which a child starts school. Although this is a form of summative assessment, the results will inform planning for the child's future learning at an individual level as well as being used to predict a child's progress and likely achievement at the end of Key Stage 1 by making comparisons with national data.

## Recording

Assessments need to be recorded in order to be useful and you need to select what to record, bearing in mind that your assessments will be used by others. Records of formative assessment may consist of notes, photographs and annotated pieces of work, while records of summative assessment take the form of scores, grades and levels. Some recording systems will already be in place in school but most teachers also keep records for their own use. Always be careful when making records about children and ask yourself if you would be happy for other people to read your personal records on children.

# Reporting

Society has a right to receive detailed and accurate information about the performance of our schools and education system and the standards of achievement of our learners. It is a statutory requirement that teachers report on pupils' progress at least once a year through annual reports and a meeting with parents. Mitchell and Koshy (1995) identify four criteria which you should meet when writing annual reports for parents. Reports need to be accessible and make sense to those who will be reading them. They need to go beyond generalisation and be specific about the achievements of children. They should be explicit and meaningful in relation to the National Curriculum and provide a focus for home–school partnership. Assessments must provide an effective means of communication and be meaningful to parents, teachers and other stakeholders. They must also provide information that is sufficiently precise to enable others to support children's learning.

The following case study is an example of an assessment policy. It is not intended to be exemplary. It is a working document and, as such, is subject to modification and amendment. In addition, each school will mould its policies according to the particular needs and current priorities of its teaching and learning community. Assessment policies therefore vary significantly between schools. However, it does enable you to put the theory into a school-based context.

## Case study 6.1

### Myton Primary School Assessment Policy

#### Rationale:
The aim of this policy is to set out the expectations for assessing and marking children's work at Myton Primary School and the roles and responsibilities of various members of staff involved in this process. The policy should be read in conjunction with the Assessment and Marking Guidelines. We, at Myton Primary School, believe that presentation is an important skill and although not formally assessed it is an ongoing factor in marking children's work. Display celebrates exemplary work, thus contributing to standards against which assessment is made. The Guidelines therefore incorporate presentation and display.

Accurate, intelligent, informed assessment provides valuable data for the learner in directing their own learning and the teacher in planning learning for pupils. The communication of this with the community demonstrates the school's abilities to oversee effectively, plan and develop its curriculum on both an individualised and whole-school basis.

Assessment is a continuous process by which teachers and learners find out about pupils' capabilities and achievements.

It is an integral part of the National Curriculum statutory procedures. This policy outlines the purpose and management of assessment in our school. The implementation of this policy is the responsibility of all staff.

## Purposes:

*Formative:* Identify future targets for the class, group and individual as appropriate within the subject areas (i.e. individual targets may well be appropriate within core subjects but not necessarily in foundation subjects).

*Diagnostic:* Identify children's strengths and weaknesses.

*Summative:* Monitor children's progress.

*Ipsative:* Commenting on work in relation to children's individual prior achievement.

Assessment can be used:

- to inform parents of their children's progress
- to promote continuity and progression between year groups
- to ensure a consistent approach to judging children's attainment
- to support children's achievement and progress
- to ensure that assessment opportunities are not missed and that the outcomes of assessment are used in the planning of future work
- to inform future planning and school development
- to identify and support special needs
- to provide information to external auditors
- to support the professional development of teachers
- to assist in evaluating the success of curriculum delivery
- to encourage teacher reflection as to the appropriateness of teaching styles employed.

### Marking

Marking is a fundamental element of the assessment process. It is central to short-term and ongoing formative assessment. Marking should provide positive reinforcement, highlighting and encouraging commendable aspects of work and setting aims to demonstrate to learners where and how their work could be extended and improved.

Children should be encouraged to mark and check their own work. Teaching children to mark their own work is an integral part of the learning process and fosters independent learning in all subjects. It also enables teachers to focus on higher-order skills when marking. All recorded work must be checked by the teacher directing the group or class. The level of detail will vary from day to day. Teachers should ensure that all children's work reflects a similar level of marking detail over a period of time.

Work should be marked as soon as possible after its completion, preferably the same day, but no later than one week after the work was done. In order to be effective, marking should be consistent throughout the school. Presentation should also be marked according to agreed guidelines (see Marking Code in Appendix).

### Schedule of assessments

### Short-term assessments

*Daily and weekly assessments*  For most National Curriculum subjects the school will follow QCA and the NNS guidance that states that schools should only collect assessment information on children who achieve beyond or below that of the majority of pupils. The school will assess all foundation subjects on that basis.

These records do not need to be detailed but should provide enough information for the teacher to:

- show progress over time;
- accurately complete end-of-year reports to parents;
- record significant achievements; and
- level the child against National Curriculum criteria.

*Tests*  All children should have weekly tests of their spelling and the rapid recall of mental arithmetic.

*Other*  Teachers cannot realistically record everything. Other forms of short-term assessments, therefore, should be used at the teacher's discretion and do not necessarily need recording.

### Medium-term assessments

Children's attainment in foundation subjects will be assessed at the end of each unit and recorded on the QCA unit sheets. Numeracy will be assessed using the relevant scheme's assessment sheets for the preceding half-term. English is assessed by levelling a piece of writing for each child. Data will be entered into the QCA record sheets/relevant tracking documents and one copy kept for the class records, one copy passed to the relevant subject co-ordinator and one copy passed to the Assessment Co-ordinator.

### Long-term assessments

Long-term assessments are conducted in order to monitor children's progress and achievement in relation to targets and to identify any 'gaps' in achievement which may require additional input from teaching staff.

Children are assessed at the end of September using the:

NFER English;

NFER Maths; and

NFER Spelling.

These tests enable a prediction to be made as to the likely SAT score which each child will achieve.

In May, Yr3, Yr4 and Yr5 undertake QCA optional SATs and are teacher-assessed against the National Curriculum Level Descriptors.

## Statutory assessment

### 1. Teacher assessment

For each child in the final year of Key Stage 2, teacher and test assessments must be made of the level achieved in each of the attainment targets in English, Maths and Science. Teacher assessments in these subjects must be completed in the summer term. Teacher assessments in all applicable attainment targets must be made continuously throughout Key Stage 2. For pupils who move to a new school other than at the end of a key stage, the current requirement is to provide the receiving school with the latest TA levels for all attainment targets in English, Maths and Science. Records of assessment in core subjects will be passed on to the next teacher / school at the time of transfer.

### 2. SATs

All children in Year 6 will undertake SATs testing. The school will seek to have children with SEN disapplied from the tests if it would be extremely difficult for the child to attempt any of the questions.

Children may have special arrangements for SATs tests and these will be conducted according to QCA's guidelines.

The organisation and administering of testing is the responsibility of all Year 6 teachers. During the testing period, Year 6 will have priority for available room space.

Records of assessment in core subjects will be passed on to the next teacher / school at time of transfer.

## Portfolios

Co-ordinators will collect samples of work to develop a portfolio from all areas of their curriculum subject and for all ability ranges. This will be used to support teachers' National Curriculum levelling. These will be developed in Maths and Science in the year 2002–3. Foundation subject and ICT portfolios will be developed in 2003–4.

The head teacher and co-ordinators will set up yearly cross-moderation staff meetings to ensure consistency of teacher assessments for children working at National Curriculum levels in Maths, Language and Science.

## Targets

Evidence from assessments should form the basis of individual targets. These targets should be set within the first four weeks of each term and should be achievable within that term. Children should be involved as far as possible in the target-setting process.

Once targets are achieved, children should be set new targets, but all targets should be reviewed as an ongoing process.

### Collection and analysis of data

A variety of sources of data will be used to analyse the progress of individual children, year groups and the whole school. At present the school uses SATs test results, PANDA reports, LEA reports and QCA reports (e.g. 'Standards at Key Stage 2') to:

- analyse the progress of teaching and learning in maths, science, reading and writing within the whole school;
- identify the type of problems that children find difficult/easy;
- identify weaknesses and strengths in relation to other local schools with a similar intake; and
- identify areas of weakness and strength nationally.

This information is then used to develop a focus in planning, teaching and INSET.

In addition to this test data, the school is developing ways of tracking pupil's achievement over a year in Maths, English and Science by using teacher assessment against SAT level descriptors and data from the optional SATs. The data will be entered and collected on class assessment sheets (see Appendix) by teachers and passed on to the assessment co-ordinator and relevant subject co-ordinator for analysis. The detailed arrangements for monitoring are set out in the Guidelines.

### Review of attainment

Each term the class teacher meets with the SENCO to review the progress of each child in the class, not just those on the SEN register. Children whose progress, behaviour or attitude is a cause of concern, or who have exhibited particular strengths, are highlighted. These children may be placed on the SEN register at School Action if they are not already on the register.

### Informing parents

Parents need to be fully informed of all aspects of their child's education. We will ensure parents are informed by:

- holding a 'Meet the Teacher' night with parents at the beginning of the year to discuss expectations, topics and timetables;
- meeting informally with parents at the end of the day to discuss how their child is doing and any concerns they/we might have;

- ensuring parents feel welcome to discuss their child's progress;

- meeting with parents whose child is on the SEN register; and

- meeting with parents at the end of the year to discuss the child's report and arrangements for the forthcoming year.

Each year a detailed report will be written about each child's progress, attainment, acquisition of skills and knowledge and their social and emotional development. Reports should provide information for parents and the child's future teacher.

## Appendix: Guidelines

These guidelines provide detailed information on the implementation of the Assessment and Marking Policy, and should be read in conjunction with that document.

### *Monitoring of assessments*

### Short-term

Co-ordinators will conduct work surveys in their subject once a term of six books/observations from each class to ensure teachers are following relevant assessment policy. The HT may also make periodic checks on class assessment and work books to ensure short-term assessment policies are being followed.

### Medium-term

At the beginning of each term co-ordinators should monitor the work of three children from each class for evidence of achievement at the teacher's assessed level. The HT may also make periodic checks to ensure medium-term assessment policies are being followed.

### Long-term

SATs and optional SATs will be conducted each year.

### Assessment sheets

Assessment collection sheets will serve a variety of purposes for different members of staff. They should support teachers in:

- levelling children against National Curriculum criteria;

- identifying key elements of progression;

- collecting information efficiently;

- setting targets for individual children;

- planning future class work; and

- writing end-of-year reports.

They should support the co-ordinators and HT in:

- allowing efficient collection of data so that whole-school progress can be measured;

- identifying the distribution of attainment in different classes;

- identifying the relative attainment of boys and girls;

- identifying which classes have a disproportionate number of children who are not attaining at expected levels, so that support can be focused; and

- identifying the accuracy of teacher assessments.

## Marking guidelines

Marking may focus on context and be diagnostic and it will give children feedback on their progress and response to work. Feedback includes writing positive comments and giving stickers or stamps for good work. Teachers will choose their own preferred reward system for their own teaching groups. Marking should also go beyond this to indicate to children how their work could be improved. Such marking should generally relate to the teaching focus, or to errors a child should not be making. For example, if the focus of a piece of writing was describing a setting, or using connectives, then marking comments should focus on these points. However, the teacher may also draw attention to careless errors, e.g. in spellings, punctuation or handwriting, which the child should be getting right routinely. These errors can be underlined or circled to show the child that they need to be checked. Other comments may include a reminder or suggestion, e.g. 'Remember to check for full stops' or 'Think of some different words for "said".' Some comments should indicate why a piece of work is good, for example, 'Good, you can write the letter h the right way now', or 'Well done for remembering to use words like "but", "next", "suddenly", instead of just using "and then".' Such comments will encourage children to continue to work at this level and will also communicate teacher expectations. Although the tone of marking over time should be positive and give suggestions for improvement, teachers should not accept work below the  standard they would normally expect from a child and should investigate the reasons for underachievement with the child.

Children should learn how to mark or check their own work. The focus of this may vary from checking punctuation or common spellings to checking for particular elements linked to the content of a lesson, e.g. using different connectives. Children could refer to checklists that remind them what they must check by themselves before giving work to the teacher to be marked. Teaching children to check their own work is an integral part of the learning process in all subjects. As well as encouraging children to take responsibility for the general standard of their work, it enables teachers to focus on higher-level skills when marking.

## The marking code

Teachers should use their judgement about which parts of the code are appropriate for the age and ability of the children they are teaching.

Marking should be done with a coloured pen (other than black/blue) so that it is easily visible to children.

Teachers may add information that might include:

- a record of the child's response to the task;

- the context of the task;

- the level of independence and adult support; and

- the adult working with the child (e.g. a signature).

## Reports

One copy should be sent home and the other retained at school and filed in the child's records at the end of the year. Parents have an opportunity to discuss the report with the class teacher during the summer parent consultation evening. Comments in reports should be specific and give parents information about what children have learnt, the progress made over the year and how the child is doing in comparison with other children.

Jargon, acronyms or other abbreviations (e.g. IEP) should be avoided, but educational terms should be used where necessary.

Reports will be completed on a computer template. Reports must have correct spellings and grammar. Reports where mistakes are frequent or where errors cannot be corrected easily will be returned for rewriting.

It is helpful to indicate to parents what the child needs to practise and how this can be supported or encouraged at home.

## Foundation subjects

Teachers may:

- comment on topics done and the understanding the child has demonstrated;

- refer to trips etc., illustrating how these contributed to the child's learning;

- indicate type of work done and comment on a child's development of particular skills and knowledge;

- comment on a child's interest and involvement, e.g. 'has learnt about . . . can . . . knows how to . . .', etc.;

- comment on participation and willingness;

- indicate level of competence, e.g. co-ordination, control, awareness of space and creativity in PE; and

- if necessary, comment on whether children have been bringing appropriate clothing for PE.

When discussing reports with parents, emphasise the importance of this area for the child's general development and wellbeing. Be positive, but honest – if there is a concern, inform the parents.

*Attendance*

It is a legal requirement to report the percentage of time a child has attended. This figure will be calculated and entered (with a comment if necessary) by the head teacher. If factors such as poor attendance, lateness or extended leave have affected the child's progress, teachers should make this clear in the report.

*Evaluations*

## Weekly

Children's response to tasks set during the week can be recorded on the evaluation section of the planning sheets to inform future planning, or in any other way that is manageable and accessible.

Evaluation comments are particularly useful for recording children's response to practical activities.

## Termly

Teachers should evaluate work undertaken during the term on the termly planning sheets. This should indicate what tasks were undertaken and which parts of the plan were changed and why. It should also indicate which activities worked well and which were problematic and why this was the case.

## Yearly

At the end of the year staff will evaluate the work undertaken by the pupils and alterations will be made to the schemes of work if necessary.

*Presentation*

## Aims:

- to achieve consistency in the way children present written work throughout the school; and

- to communicate to children that we expect high standards in the presentation of work.

## Dating work

All work should be dated. Children should be taught how to write the date themselves, at least using the short form, e.g. 5/2/05.

Children should also know how to write the longer form, spelling the days and months.

## Underlining titles

Where lines are drawn children must use rulers. Children should be taught how to draw lines using a ruler in Year 3 and should be competent doing so in Year 4. Borders or decorations should not be drawn around titles or other parts of work (except in particular circumstances where decoration or illustration is part of the work).

## Use of rubbers

Errors should be crossed through with a single stroke or line. Rubbers may be used occasionally at the teacher's discretion if this improves the overall standard of work.

## Spacing work

When using exercise books children should not leave pages or large amounts of blank space. A small space or two to three lines can be left between one piece of work and another (unless the finished work is near the end of a page).

## Book covers

Covers of books should be kept clean and children should not draw or scribble on them. If children do so they should be asked to erase the scribbles.

### Handwriting

Children should follow the school scheme of writing in all of their workbooks. Letters formed differently to this should be corrected in books. Children must use lined paper or guidelines when writing, to encourage correct formation of letters with ascenders and descenders. Errors in these should be corrected.

### Display

It is important to display children's writing and recording from a range of curriculum areas. As well as acknowledging children's achievement, displays can be used to model the standards we expect and to highlight particularly good features of children's work. Work from children of different abilities should be displayed but within the context of what children are capable of doing the work should meet the requirements of this policy. Teachers should not display work that is clearly below the standard which a child is capable of producing.

To work effectively, displays must be attractive and indicate clearly the context and purpose of the work. Teachers' labels should explain or give information about the work. Labels can also be used to acknowledge particular achievement or to emphasise a teaching point, e.g. 'Azim has remembered to use capital letters; James has used some interesting words to describe the monster, gigantic, terrifying, wrinkly', etc.

Work displayed does not always have to be the final or finished product. In writing, for example, it can be useful to display the different stages of writing, e.g. planning, first draft etc. Likewise, in art or technology less successful first attempts, displayed alongside final pieces, can make a useful teaching point, especially if accompanied by an explanation of how the improvements were made.

# Conclusion

This chapter, along with Chapter 5, has shown you how the planning and assessment cycle works for the benefit of your pupils' learning. It is important that you build assessment opportunities into your planning right from the outset.

# Suggestions for further reading

Black, P. and Wiliam, D. (1998) *Inside the Black Box*. London: King's College.

This book describes a very interesting study that sets out to explore how formative assessment contributes to effective teaching. The 'black box' of the title is the classroom, and the authors seek to discover what happens in the box to create the outputs that we want. *Inside the Black Box* proposes several ways to improve formative assessment.

Pollard, A. (ed.) (1996) *Readings for Reflective Teaching in the Primary School*. London: Cassell.

# References

Assessment Reform Group (2002) *Principles of Assessment for Learning,* http://www.assessment-reform-group.org.uk

DfEE/QCA (1999) *The National Curriculum: Handbook for Primary Teachers in England: Key Stages 1 and 2.* London: DfEE.

Mitchell, C. and Koshy, V. (1995) *Effective Teacher Assessment: Looking at Children's Learning in the Primary Classroom* (2nd edn). London: Hodder and Stoughton.

Pollard, A. (ed.) (1996) *Readings for Reflective Teaching in the Primary School*. London: Cassell.

# Behaviour management

## Teresa Leggett

## Introduction

> 3 September 2003 – The class were rioting – climbing walls, escaping through the windows and generally being very rowdy. My frantic appeals for order died unheeded and I ended up hunched on the floor in the middle of the classroom, weeping, while the little darlings mocked me.

Thankfully this was only a dream – the same one I have every year before returning to school after the summer break. It is rooted only in my subconscious and has never been a reality.

Effective behaviour management is essential for the smooth running of your classroom. Bearing this in mind, it has not always been high on the agenda in teacher training institutions. The advice I remember being given was limited – there was one lesson observation feedback form that read 'Try to avoid using sarcasm and the temptation to shout'. There was also the cynical pensioner who told us, with alarming regularity, not to smile until Christmas. I am sure this is no longer the case, but behaviour management is still an issue that concerns all teachers, not just those new to the profession.

## Activity 7.1

Observe different teachers at work. How do they create a positive climate for learning? How do they prevent bad behaviour?

## Whole-school policy – positive discipline

There is no doubt that a positive school ethos, which actively promotes respect for one another and a supportive learning environment, has a significant impact on standards of behaviour within a school. The ethos of the school is created by all those who work in it and a cohesive and shared ethos is essential.

All schools need a behaviour policy that operates throughout the school if behaviour management is to be effective and facilitate a meaningful learning environment. However, no matter how good whole-school policy may be, it can only work when all staff, both teaching and non-teaching, promote the policy in practice, and children understand the way in which systems work and the objectives behind them. It is important to follow school guidelines for rewarding good behaviour and adhere to established consequences for unacceptable behaviour. A number of programmes are used to this end. Perhaps the most popular is the Assertive Discipline Programme.

## Assertive discipline

Many schools today have taken on board the Assertive Discipline model advocated by Marlene and Lee Canter (2001) and have adopted this model effectively to create productive whole-school behaviour management strategies. More commonly, this model has been adapted to meet the needs of the school. Marlene and Lee Canter spent thousands of hours observing teachers at work and based their model on successful practice. Their aim was to create a model that created an environment where teachers can teach and students can learn. The Canters advocate that a positive approach to discipline creates a climate of positive support that appreciates and rewards those who conform, while maintaining firm control over the students. Assertive discipline is a structured, systematic approach designed to assist teachers and teaching assistants in running a classroom where the teacher has control but does not stifle creativity and exploration.

## Good relationships are central to effective behaviour management

The Assertive Discipline model is dependent upon clear lines of communication between child and teacher. Teachers must make their expectations clear to children and parents. Good relationships, based on mutual respect, will be promoted when children feel their needs are being met within a safe and structured environment. Children need firm boundaries within which to operate. At the start of each year it is important to spend time with a new class establishing a code of conduct for the classroom; this must be in line with whole-school behaviour policies but must also meet the needs of the children in the class. If children take ownership of these they are more likely to respond positively towards them.

It is imperative that you, as the teacher, take time to get to know the children you teach. All children are individuals with their own needs and idiosyncrasies – because of extraneous factors the way in which you deal with behaviour issues may need to vary from one child to the next. In order to build good relationships the teacher should not try to be the child's best friend; in fact this is counter-productive. Children need to feel secure and understand the barriers. A friend was talking recently about taking his eleven-year-old daughter to an open evening at secondary school. He spoke of how he was disturbed by the 'hell and damnation' speech made by the head on what happens to those who fail to conform to school rules and was afraid that his daughter's enthusiasm for her move to a new school would be crushed. He was surprised when he turned to her and could see the tension visibly fade from her face. She was relieved to hear that the bullies she had heard so much about would be dealt with. Good relationships are built on a foundation of many factors – as far as she was concerned the school cared about her happiness and right to a good education in a safe environment. The children must feel that they can trust their teacher: if you are seen to be fair, consistent and approachable, most children will want to behave well for you, thus making your task significantly easier. The child who feels that you are interested in him/her and value his/her progress will be far more co-operative than the child who feels insignificant. I have seen really difficult children crumble when a teacher they truly respect has said to them 'I'm very disappointed in you'.

Teachers must be consistent in their approach to behaviour management – expectations need to be made clear to the children and then made explicit through practice. Children, for example, need to be aware that you expect them to listen when you or somebody else is talking; if you then talk over them they will begin to question your authority and you will fail to gain their respect.

Good behaviour needs to be valued. When observing teachers interacting with children it is common to see teachers rewarding good behaviour in those who frequently misbehave, but far less common to see teachers rewarding those who always conform to codes of conduct; it is therefore important to create systems which will allow you to reward good behaviour in all children. Many schools have their own systems of rewards and these should be adhered to, but rewards such as table of the day, pupil of the week, stars and stickers work well with most children. Those systems that involve the children working collaboratively are generally most effective.

Unfortunately, from time to time, I have come across teachers who believe that humiliation is an effective way of maintaining a controlled learning environment. Humiliation, especially when done publicly, will only serve to disaffect children and will break down rather than build up positive relationships. Rogers (1995) reiterates this, citing research documented in the Elton Report (DES 1989), claiming that humiliation breeds resentment and 'poisons a school's atmosphere'. It is easy to humiliate children without meaning to: 'You have a go at this easier worksheet'. This, said to a child in front of peers, is not going to foster the type of relationship that will encourage the child to have a positive attitude to school life and learning.

## Activity 7.2

Look at reward systems used in classrooms. Develop a bank of systems you could use. Different strategies work with different classes. You need to be flexible.

## Building self-esteem

I strongly believe that many children who behave badly suffer from poor levels of self-esteem and use poor behaviour in an attempt to distract from perceived areas of weakness and as a means of gaining favour with peers. Informal research in and beyond the classroom has shown a direct link between those children identified by staff as being badly behaved and those children who gain low scores in self-esteem questionnaires. This, therefore, impacts directly on what we as teachers do in the classroom. Through praise and encouragement we can have a real impact upon children's belief in themselves and this should impact on how we talk to children about their work and their skills. Finding opportunities to praise children is important – this praise must be genuine and children can tell the difference between a glib 'Wow, that's really good. Now get on with the next bit' and a genuine appreciation of their achievements. Some teachers use praise too freely and it becomes meaningless. In general, children can cope with constructive criticism if they know you will be pleased when they achieve their goal. I once taught a child who exhibited very challenging behaviour. I discovered in him a talent for drama and persuaded his mother to enrol him in a drama club, where he was able to achieve success. This had an amazing impact on his behaviour in school – the confidence and self-esteem he gained there reflected in his approach to school life.

## Lessons must be well planned

I hear the groans – just when you thought you had found a chapter where the importance of planning would not raise its ugly head, it does, and I make no apologies for it because careful and considered lesson planning that builds upon prior experiences and differentiates to meet the needs of all pupils is central to effective behaviour management. Children who are actively engaged in stimulating and meaningful lessons are far less likely to be disruptive than those who are bored and alienated from learning. It is important to set the tone of the lesson by being in the classroom to meet and greet the pupils. Teachers are actors who need to stimulate interest and engagement in learning. If activities do not challenge the children or are too hard behaviour may become disruptive; therefore careful differentiation is paramount to a purposeful learning environment. Children need to be able to work independently while you focus your time on a target group. You need to ensure that this is possible.

Behaviour management becomes more difficult if there is a group of children who cannot access learning during whole-class sessions. They become frustrated and even more disaffected. All children need to feel involved and it is important to build in opportunities for all children to be actively engaged.

We all remember the teacher who never marked our work and who quite evidently had not got the foggiest idea who we were or what we were capable of. We can also recollect the impact this had on our own motivation. While marking books can sometimes be the straw that breaks the camel's back at the end of a long and tiring day, it is important that children get feedback on their work. If we do not value a child's efforts why should they make the effort?

## Classroom organisation

I constantly change the way in which my classroom is organised in order to meet the needs of the children I am teaching at the time. However, whatever the age of the children, I always ensure I have a carpet space where I can sit the children around me. I generally find this the most effective way of class teaching – the children are closer to you so are naturally more attentive. You also need to create as much space as possible. In many schools the teaching space is far too small. For most of us, moving walls is beyond our realm of expertise; we are, however, capable of furniture removal and, while it is ideal to have spare tables for display and cupboards for resources, if space is an issue they must go. The caretaker will doubtless mumble under his breath about how the last teacher managed for years with bigger classes than you've got, but don't be put off, because if you are going to have to shoe-horn the pupils into their seats in September the problems next July are going to be insurmountable. If the children do not have sufficient personal space they become short-tempered; they knock one another and this soon becomes perceived as purposeful, causing conflict that can escalate. Seating is an important issue in classroom organisation; I like to seat children in ability groups as it is easier to work with focused groups. However, if two children of similar ability are sworn enemies this will not work – it may be necessary to subdivide that group into two groups and pull the tables together when you want to work with them as a unit. Many students and NQTs who experience difficulties with behaviour management do so because they do not ensure that they can always see all the children. If the children are aware that you are watching they are far less likely to misbehave and go off-task.

It is important that children can access resources without having to wait for you – a child having to ask you for another piece of paper is off-task; resources should be readily available, well-stocked and labelled.

## Be there

As I have already mentioned, you need to be 'omnipresent' in the classroom; your presence needs to be felt even when you are working quietly with a group. I recall a child who described me as having ears everywhere and eyes in my back. 'How does she know?' he asked.

After many years of working with students and NQTs I can now make quite accurate judgements about a teacher's effectiveness in the classroom before seeing them work with children – this isn't because I have some sort of sixth sense but because effective teachers, who are able to create purposeful learning environments, are rarely shrinking violets. Teachers are actors – they exude enthusiasm and commitment. This does not mean that naturally quiet people do not make good teachers and the loud and brash excel in the profession – those who make excellent teachers know when to adopt a calm and quiet approach and when to become more animated and flamboyant. As teachers we need to inspire children to learn, engage their interest and motivate them to meet challenges; this is most effectively managed when teachers vary their presentation style and voice. Teachers who never get out of their seat or get excited about what they are teaching do not inspire children to learn. However, those who never stand still and are always very enthusiastic can be quite daunting, especially for a more timid child. The key is to balance your approach to match the learning outcomes and activity.

## But what do I do when they don't behave?

However good your behaviour management there will be times when children do not conform, and you have to deal with incidences of unacceptable behaviour. Many of these will probably occur in the playground. There is very little you can do to stop this happening. I used to believe, naïvely, that I could build bridges between children who disliked one another; I now realise that this is neither possible nor fair on the children. I now insist they stay away from one another and help them to find new friendship groups if necessary. This is far more effective.

I have already mentioned the importance for you to be 'omnipresent' in the classroom – ensuring you can see all children at all times will allow you to anticipate bad behaviour and distract the child; for example, pulling the inattentive child back into a whole-class session by targeting a question at them or getting a child back on task by reaffirming their target for the lesson in terms of work output.

Teachers who blame the whole class for an individual or group's misbehaviour will soon lose the respect of the class. It is important that the correct culprit is punished, not the whole class. We all remember the time the entire class lost playtime because 'there is too much noise in this room' and the injustice we felt at this; your class will feel equally aggrieved. A friend's six-year-old son once came home from school very indignant – 'My teacher sees with her ears not her eyes,' he said. 'We all lost golden time because somebody was shouting. How fair's that?' Inappropriate behaviour can disrupt the flow of a lesson, impacting on the quality of teaching and learning afforded to the class. It is best to deal with the situation and leave discussion until later. 'Stop that, Johnny. We'll talk about it later' or 'Come over here and sit by me, Johnny. I'll talk to you at break time' is far less disruptive than a full discussion with Johnny about the error of his ways that will mean the flow of the lesson is interrupted. Quite often disruptions can be dealt with using non-verbal communication. As a young teacher I can remember being appalled by teachers who clicked their fingers and pointed, thinking it incredibly rude, but it's a technique I now use frequently and with much success. When somebody once told me that the best way to deal with unacceptable behaviour was to use soft words and strong arguments I struggled to understand them. However, the wisdom of these words changed the way in which I dealt with incidences of non-conformity dramatically and has been very effective. I realise now that my approach, particularly with those who had been bullying others, used to be rather aggressive; it is now assertive. An aggressive approach makes the child scared of repeating this behaviour if they think you are likely to find out and carry out your threats but will not change their behaviour, whereas an assertive approach will involve discussion with the child and enable them to see the effect their behaviour is having on others. I still make it very clear to the child that I do not like their behaviour and will not tolerate it, but I attempt to change this behaviour through reasoned discussion rather than scare the child into not doing it again.

When dealing with a child who is agitated or aggressive it is important to avoid confrontation – staying calm will put you in a position of control. As Cowley (2003) points out, it is very difficult to argue with someone who won't argue back and this will soon diffuse the situation.

I emphasise again the importance of following school policy in dealing with inappropriate behaviour. Children will test a new teacher and even conformists will push the boundaries if they sense a weakness; just as a horse will be skittish and disobedient for an experienced rider, so will a child for an unassertive teacher who does not apply policy consistently.

## Activity 7.3

Observe a child with behaviour problems for a day – note incidences of bad behaviour and how these are dealt with or could have been prevented.

## Working with parents

It is important to create a positive and open relationship with parents, as their support in dealing with behaviour issues is invaluable. Efforts should be made to inform parents of the good as well as the bad – postcards and certificates taken home, even stickers on a jumper, create a good rapport. A word at the school gate praising work or behaviour makes you more approachable, and this is important as it will make breaking negative news much easier. As soon as there is any deterioration in a child's behaviour or attitude to school, I would advocate talking to parents. An informal chat is often all that is necessary and parents normally appreciate the opportunity to discuss these issues with you. When children know that home and school are working together there is often an immediate improvement. If a parent's only involvement is a letter telling them their child is at risk of exclusion they are more likely to be defensive and aggressive. Talking

## Case study 7.1

The aim here is not to scare but to reassure – it is possible to survive unscathed a year with a very difficult class providing the school has in place structures to support you.

The school in which I am currently working is in an ex-mining village in the north-east of County Durham. The class who will form the foundation for the case study are the most challenging group I have come across in my many years in primary education. A class of 20 Year 6 children on the face of it seems idyllic, but all of the children presented problems that made this a very difficult and challenging group to teach. To counteract this the level of job satisfaction was tremendous as I watched many of them mature and blossom under a very structured regime. At some point you will meet this class – if you are unlucky it will be in your first year of teaching.

The school has a very structured and well-considered behaviour policy that was written in consultation with all stakeholders: teachers, non-teaching staff, children, parents and governors. It is centred on a code of conduct, and rewards good behaviour while highlighting consequences for those who don't conform. All staff are aware of procedures and follow them consistently throughout the school. If this were not the case, the systems would break down and the purposeful and secure learning environment created in the school would not exist. However, despite these systems there are still times when behaviour is inappropriate and needs to be dealt with. The focus children had caused problems throughout their time in school and the senior management team took the unprecedented decision to organise the two Year 6 classes according to behaviour, the aim being to create one class that would allow the children who always conformed to have an enjoyable year in an environment which would encourage them to be creative and meet their full potential, and another that would provide a very structured environment with high expectations of behaviour, with programmes in place to promote self-esteem. The children presented a range of behaviour issues that needed to be addressed. A number of the children were on the child protection register or categorised as children in need and therefore a multi-agency approach was necessary to meet their needs. Others were immature and demonstrated poor concentration skills, and many of the children had developed a range of work avoidance strategies to cover academic difficulties. A number of the children were very aggressive towards peers and needed work on anger management.

It was important to have a very structured approach with these children, and during the summer break I spent a long time organising my classroom. The desks were arranged into a horseshoe to minimise contact between the children, and each was allocated a seat. This initially worked effectively as there were a group of children who would have caused a high level of disruption had they been able to communicate easily with one another. Later in the year they developed non-verbal systems of communication that meant I had to re-organise seating for these children so that they did not have a direct line of vision from one to the other. Discussion with the teachers who had taught the children in Year 5 was essential to effective organisation and this is true with any class, especially when you are new to the school and do not know the children well. It is always important to read children's personal files prior to teaching them as this gives you background information that will help you in not only organising your classroom but also in anticipating any problems and minimising any possibility of setting off on a bad footing. I remember in my first year of teaching asking the children on their first day to write about their mothers – nobody had thought to tell me that one child had lost her mother the year before. I caused her great distress and it took a long time to build a good relationship with her after this.

The allocation of resources also needed consideration. Under normal circumstances I would put stationery in a central box on each table, but this was not viable with a group of children who would make the most of any opportunity to bicker and fight. While I felt that I should try to teach the children to share resources, this had to be weighed against the need to provide a high-quality education that encouraged a positive work ethos in these children. To this end all children were given their own named resources including coloured pencils and a glue stick. This was costly but effective with this group of children and ensured they had to take responsibility for looking after their own equipment – this proved quite a challenge for some of them and was a good experience.

I made my expectations very clear to the children and was stringent in demanding conformity. Initially, this meant I spent many of my break times sitting with children who had not completed work or had behaved unacceptably, but this improved as the children realised I did not issue empty threats. Again, whatever your class is like, this is very important; it is no good giving children targets and not enforcing them. I was also very careful to reward good behaviour; the sweet jar was my best friend and a drain on my income, but the children appreciated the fact that I valued their efforts. Sweets are not approved of in every school, and understandably so in a climate where most schools are working to promote a healthy lifestyle, but my normal stickers and postcards home did not have the same effect as they would with most classes. When giving rewards you do need to ensure that you are not falling foul of school guidelines. Every Friday afternoon we had an awards ceremony where children were given certificates for good behaviour and improvement and this became very important to the children. I was often tempted to forgo it because of the pressures of the curriculum but the children worked towards it and felt I was letting them down if we did not complete this ritual. I made it very clear to children why I was giving a certificate and set them a target for the next week. Most children were quite upset if they did not receive a certificate. Parents also became involved and many children received treats for taking home a certificate and this was a good way of maintaining home–school contact. Added to this, I operated a merit system where children were given stamps for positive behaviour and work, and were awarded bronze, silver and gold awards for meeting targets.

Most children responded positively to this structure and developed a more positive attitude to work and the structures of school life. However, there was still a minority of children who either could not or did not want to conform. These children continued to behave in an inappropriate manner. Their behaviour had to be managed if the class was to function properly and this was done with the support of the head teacher and colleagues. Individual behaviour programmes were set with these children and their parents. The LEA behaviour support team was also involved, offering support and advice on behaviour management strategies. They also provided intervention programmes on behaviour management for a number of children. The behaviour programmes involved the children in earning privileges, such as playing for the football team and going on a school trip. This worked effectively where parents were supportive, but when parents failed to support the school the programmes had only a short-term and limited effect. If children were too disruptive in class they were removed to work in other classrooms or with the head teacher. This allowed the rest of the class to operate productively.

The teaching of Personal, Social, Health and Citizenship Education is considered very important throughout the school but became particularly important with these children. The normal PSHCE curriculum was taught but was supplemented with a self-esteem programme, aimed at encouraging children to recognise their own strengths and appreciate the impact that their actions can have on those around them and in the wider community. The Pathways Project involved children working in small groups to complete a range of activities. This involved a number of adults and only worked because the head teacher and a very experienced and skilled learning support assistant were involved. However, baseline and summative assessments suggested that for most children the project had a positive impact.

These strategies worked with most of the children – they had a good year and made good progress. It didn't work with them all, and towards the end of the year two of the children were given fixed-term exclusions. As a young teacher I would have felt I had failed; with experience and wisdom I have learnt to look at the positive – the majority of children blossomed in some way over the year.

Many of these strategies will be effective with any class and I have learnt much from working with this class that will impact on my practice in future. Most significantly, it raised my awareness of the positive impact of creating opportunities to offer children genuine praise; this also allows you to set targets in a very positive atmosphere.

to parents can be quite a daunting task for NQTs and it is advisable to ask a senior member of staff to see parents with you, especially if the parent is known to be unco-operative.

Home–school diaries are an effective way of maintaining contact between home and school when trying to modify a child's behaviour.

## Conclusion

> It is a mistake to view discipline as something concerned with how you deal with pupil misbehaviour, separate from your general teaching. (Kyriacou 1991: 81)

I hope this chapter has shown you that good classroom management is firmly embedded in a whole-school policy and structures that both you and the children understand. It is not just about dealing with bad behaviour but about knowing your children, making their learning exciting and motivating and ensuring that strategies for rewarding good behaviour are an important part of your classroom management.

## Suggestions for further reading

Cowley, S. (2003) *Getting the Buggers to Behave 2*. London: Continuum.

This is a very accessible book with tips for controlling your class. As well as discussing the use of sanctions and awards it also considers different teaching styles in terms of classroom management.

Roffey, S. (2004) *The New Teacher's Survival Guide to Behaviour*. London: Paul Chapman Publishing.

This is a very practical book that helps the new teacher establish and maintain positive relationships with children and so enjoy teaching.

Rogers, B. (2002) *Classroom Behaviour: A Practical Guide to Effective Teaching, Behaviour Management and Colleague Support*. London: Paul Chapman Publishing.

This is another extremely helpful book that, among many other tips and pieces of advice, addresses the management of anger (yours as well as theirs).

## References

Canter, L. and Canter, M. (2001) *Assertive Discipline: Positive Behaviour Manangement in Today's Classroom* (3rd edn). Los Angeles, CA: Canter and Associates.

Cowley, S. (2003) *Getting the Buggers to Behave 2*. London: Continuum.

DES (1989) *Discipline in Schools* (The Elton Report). London: Department for Education and Science.

Kyriacou, (1991) *Essential Teaching Skills*. Oxford: Blackwell.

Rogers, B. (1995) *Behaviour Manangement: A Whole-school Approach*. London: Paul Chapman Publishing.

# 8

# Classroom approaches and organisation

Catherine Worton

## Introduction

Children acquire new knowledge, skills and concepts in many different ways and the successful teacher is one who is well informed about the learning process. With this insight he or she should be able to select or design powerful learning experiences for pupils. However, these experiences will have little or no impact if they are presented inappropriately, organised carelessly or managed badly. In the most effective teaching there is a symbiotic relationship between the content of a lesson and its execution.

Edwards (2004) identifies three aspects of the challenge facing the teacher as he or she plans for children's learning. These are the diverse student population, the physical learning space and the routines of the classroom. Bearing this in mind, the teacher will need to select teaching techniques and organisational models that accommodate the range of abilities and personalities in the teaching group, that are manageable within the available space and that are in sympathy with routines known to pupils in the group. This selection and matching process is a complex and demanding task and is both the art and the science of teaching.

## A range of approaches

Primary education is a field of competing pedagogies and the inexperienced teacher will encounter a range of approaches among settings and colleagues. Some of these approaches may be the expression of explicit philosophies and hark back to significant educational thinkers or researchers. Other approaches may be more evolutionary in nature, consisting of structures and tasks a practitioner has observed as being successful over a period of time. More commonly, approaches are combinations of both of these. In Yapp's (1987) amusing and ironic review of the teaching profession he suggests eight classroom approaches: *tinker, tailor, soldier, sailor, rich man, poor man, beggar man* and *thief*, and, while these are caricatures, there is a good deal of truth in his descriptions. In most cases experienced practitioners will explain and defend their approach in absolute terms, leaving their new colleague lost in a maze of visionary zeal, personal anecdote, received wisdom and cynical survival tactics.

A new teacher is in a very vulnerable position in his or her first post. It is importantto be seen to be successful and in control from the outset in the eyes of pupils, parentsand colleagues. A tempting survival technique is to adopt wholesale the approach and organisational model of a colleague viewed as a competent practitioner. Smith and Coldron (1999) provide an interesting discussion of the value of observation of colleagues. It can be a highly effective technique, allowing the less-experienced educationalist to model him/herself on the successful and accomplished practitioner while opening up opportunities for professional dialogue. There are, however, some risks involved in this strategy. First, the new teacher may take a little time to realise that the success witnessed among colleagues owes less to their declared approach than to their underlying competence as experienced professionals. Thus aspects of an approach of an experienced colleague which are replicated without an understanding of rationale and without the self-belief and status of the established practitioner may fail, leaving the new teacher casting around for a new panacea to his or her problems of organisation and management. Secondly, new teachers are at risk of unconsciously absorbing less successful or undesirable aspects of practice, which their inexperience prevents them from identifying in the overall package. Thirdly, and perhaps most importantly, a slavish acceptance of a received model will make the new teacher less accepting of other approaches and stultify professional development.

How, then, does the new teacher decide which approaches to use? There is a vast amount of literature in this area including research reports, government directives and overt propaganda and it is quickly apparent that different views are dominant at various points in time and in various places. This discussion is not the place for an extended historical overview of classroom approaches. However, the new teacher should be aware of some key readings in the field. The Plowden Report (1967), the great cornerstone of primary school progressivism, promoted a social constructivist curriculum with a strong emphasis on collaborative group work. Teaching approaches were to be responsive to both the needs and interests of pupils and the teacher was to act as a facilitator to further learning. The curriculum was to be flexible and an integrated day was favoured over whole-class subject timetabling. During the early and mid-1970s the Plowden model was attacked by right-wing thinkers, who claimed that progressive ideas were detrimental to pupil progress. An important figure in this field was Neville Bennett, whose *Teaching Styles and Pupil Progress* (1976) highlighted the weaknesses of alternative approaches and organisational strategies. His views were expanded in *The Quality of Pupil Learning Experiences* (1984). Significantly, he claimed that teachers found it difficult to implement progressive models effectively and that often their practice did not measure up to their progressive rhetoric.

Studies of teaching styles are always controversial because of the varying measures used for effectiveness. Some research judges a style according to pupil attainment; other studies measure teacher effectiveness in terms of observable pupil behaviour, so that it is not always easy to make any absolute judgements. Nevertheless, teaching approaches, particularly in primary schools, were now at the forefront of national debate. The control of teaching models was moving away from institutions of higher education and into the political arena. The Education Reform Act (1988), passed by a Conservative government, established a National Curriculum, which was, by definition, and by its association with a statutory testing regime, a convergent curriculum. For the first time content was prescribed in all areas, as well as some skills and processes. However, teaching approaches were only hinted at, still leaving plenty of space for individual interpretation by professionals.

It was the so-called report of the 'Three Wise Men' (Alexander *et al.* (1992)), which brought teaching style and approaches into sharper focus with its key idea of 'fitness for purpose'. *The National Strategy for Literacy* and *The National Strategy for Numeracy*, in the late 1990s, overtly stated how lessons were to be planned and delivered. In these documents the authors advocate a mixed approach including direct exposition, differentiated group work, collaborative group work and individual work. The development of the QCA Units of Work in the foundation subjects reinforced the key features of the Literacy and Numeracy Strategies in their emphasis on particular ways of presenting material, developing concepts and organising pupils. Most recently, Ofsted has raised concerns that the prescription of the Literacy and Numeracy strategies has caused a curriculum imbalance leading to a diminution of quality in the rest of the curriculum, particularly in the arts. The government has responded with *Excellence and Enjoyment* (2004), a document which refutes the belief that high academic standards are attained by a narrow curriculum and encourages a rich and balanced programme of learning in partnership with rigour in the core subjects.

Kyriacou (2001), in a very useful summary of research into effective teaching, helps us return to first principles when he observes that:

> the basic task of effective teaching is to set up a learning experience in which pupils effectively engage in the mental activity that brings about those changes in the pupils' cognitive structure which constitute the desired learning.

Regardless of political and pedagogical trends, then, the approach adopted must be suited to the aims and objectives of particular aspects of the curriculum, as well as accommodating the characteristics of the teaching group.

## Activity 8.1

Observe a lesson taught by a mentor or colleague. Find out the objectives of the lesson in advance. Consider how the activities selected help pupils reach these objectives. Do you think this was the best type of activity for these objectives? Can you think of any alternative activities that might meet the objectives more effectively?

Think about the way pupils have been organised. Why do you think this approach was chosen? Can you see any problems with this method of organisation? Can you think of any alternative ways of organising the pupils?

There are two facets to every classroom approach, namely the type of activity designed for the pupils and the ways pupils are organised. Classroom layout is derived from this organisation. We shall look at each of these in turn, considering situations for which they are appropriate.

## Styles of activity for pupils

### Listening to and participating in direct exposition

This technique involves the transfer of new knowledge, skills and concepts from a teacher to a pupil by explicit demonstration and explanation. It is characterised by controlled use of language, clarity of sequence and reiteration of key ideas from the teacher and can be didactic or interactive, although the interaction is convergent in style. The role of the pupil is to be attentive and to retain key information. Examples of direct exposition might include the demonstration of the use of a hot glue gun or the creation of a Carroll diagram using science data.

### Reinforcement tasks

In this technique pupils are provided with the opportunity to reinforce learning from direct exposition. Reinforcement exercises may be carried out individually, in ability groups or collaboratively. Examples of reinforcement tasks might include the use of small-group bingo to consolidate reading sight vocabulary or the creation of individual history timelines based on direct exposition.

### Enrichment activities

Here pupils who have demonstrated a secure grasp of the direct exposition material can also apply their skills and knowledge in new situations. If reinforcement activities rehearse key skills, knowledge and concepts, then enrichment activities deepen and embed understanding. For example, a child who has been shown the variety of sounds made by percussion instruments and who has rehearsed these sounds for himself, under direction, might then attempt to create sound effects for a story or puppet show. A child who has been shown how to total coins of various values and has practised using a worksheet might then use this skill in paying for items or giving change in a toy shop.

## Problem-solving challenges

Here pupils have to marshal their existing knowledge and skills to construct new ways of looking at a situation. If direct exposition and reinforcement are essentially convergent experiences, then problem-solving activities are divergent with the emphasis being on the process rather than the product. Pupils are actively encouraged to move away from given solutions to find their own. Examples of problem-solving tasks might include challenging pupils to create a bridge structure to hold a given weight or asking pupils to plan and create a nourishing meal for a small amount of money for a particular group.

## Organisation of pupils

### Whole-class work

In this approach the teacher addresses and organises the pupils as one homogeneous group. In a whole-class session the teacher might engage pupils in any of the activities discussed above but the pupils will work together as a large group led by the teacher or they will tackle identical tasks concurrently but individually. Characteristically, the group will participate in at least a common introduction and plenary session. This approach is relatively straightforward to manage since pupil movement is minimal and controlled by the teacher. The teacher directs events throughout, therefore reducing opportunities for inappropriate digressions or time-wasting. There are good opportunities in this model for pupils to learn from each other as the teacher can highlight examples of good work. He or she can also reiterate the lesson objectives, making sure that pupils' thinking is tightly focused. However, it can be difficult to cater for the range of abilities in this model. If the teacher sets the pace to accommodate the most able, the less-able pupils may become confused, disaffected and perhaps even disruptive. If the teacher pitches the lesson towards the middle of the class, he or she might find that the most able children dominate the session, giving competent answers within their own comfort zone. In this situation it is very easy to feel that a lesson is 'going well' when in fact the most able cohort are not challenged, the average cohort are overshadowed and the least-able cohort are not engaged. If the teacher pitches the lesson towards the least-able pupils, more-able pupils can become bored and disruptive. It can also expose differences in ability and attainment, thereby reducing the self-esteem of less-able pupils.

In whole-class work pupils typically sit on a mat facing the teacher, in rows of desks facing the teacher or in a horseshoe formation.

### Differentiated group work

Here the teacher identifies groups of pupils who have approximately the same level of attainment. Groups are given tasks matched to their abilities. All the groups tackle activities on a similar theme. The composition of the groups may change during the day depending on the area of the curriculum under study. The teacher may work intensively with one group while other groups work independently or the teacher may divide his or her time equally between the groups. The children may be working on a common task individually or on a collaborative or exploratory task. Motivation among pupils is maintained because the work is finely graded to match their ability. On the other hand, opportunities for pupils to support less-able children or to learn from the more-able are restricted. The groups can also be divisive if used permanently. If the teacher moves among the groups then pupil encounters with the teacher are often brief and low-level. If the teacher wishes to remain undisturbed with a target group he or she may set tasks for the other groups that offer no challenge, purely to prevent interruptions. Examples of differentiated group work might be a lesson to develop skimming and scanning reading techniques, in which groups use texts of varying difficulty, or a lesson on subtraction in which pupils work with numbers of varying size.

In differentiated group work pupils typically sit around tables in their ability groups, perhaps sharing resources and giving informal support to each other.

## Individual work

The timing of individual work may be controlled by the teacher to last only for one session or for a restricted number of sessions. Alternatively, individual tasks may run for longer periods of time and involve study at home. Pupils engaged in individual assignments may be working on similar tasks to their classmates in ability bands or on unrelated tasks. Individual tasks encourage independence and autonomy. Few social demands are made on the pupils, which can in turn reduce interpersonal friction. However, there is little opportunity for pupils to learn from each other, unless the teacher cites examples of successful work in direct exposition. Monitoring of pupil progress during the activity itself is time-consuming and may be superficial because the children are involved in separate tasks, but there is often written/pictorial evidence which can be assessed after the lesson and this work is particular to individuals. Examples of individual tasks might include pupils practising the technique for a backward roll, pupils writing their own version of a fairy tale or pupils researching their own family tree.

In individual work, pupils may visit particular areas of the classroom to carry out their tasks. For example, they might use the book corner for research, an ICT suite for the presentation of a project or a science corner for an experiment. Alternatively, they might have a set seat and bring appropriate resources to this seat. Individual project work requires a classroom in which various areas of the curriculum can be explored concurrently, perhaps one in which subject bays have been created.

## Collaborative group work

In this approach the teacher divides the pupils into groups according to interests, friendships or abilities. Pupils choose, or are assigned, roles within the group and a successful response to a task requires some degree of discussion and collaboration. Groups may be as small as two or as large as six. In this model significant personal and interpersonal demands are made on the pupils. They need to engage in productive rather than oppositional discussion and they need to be able to negotiate roles and responsibilities. Whitaker (1995) suggests that such group work facilitates understanding by providing maximum opportunity for pupils to talk reflectively with each other. It also promotes co-operation and mutual respect. However, collaborative group work is perhaps the most demanding of the organisational models with a high number of prerequisite skills. These skills, which include attentive listening; retention of key information; confident, articulate speaking; personal goal or target setting; and sharing of resources, may need to be addressed before truly collaborative tasks can be attempted. Children may need a high level of support to operate collaboratively. If groups are working concurrently this might place great demands on the teacher, particularly if collaboration breaks down in one or more groups. While there is the opportunity for less-able children to learn from the more-able, there is also the possibility that some children might become socially or intellectually dominant, relegating their classmates to less than satisfying subordinate roles. Other children may be happy to act as 'passengers', make a minimal contribution and not work to their full potential. This can make assessment difficult and may inhibit the progress of some individuals.

Examples of collaborative group tasks include the design of a new ball game or preparing a drama sketch to show how to respond to bullying.

## Selecting activities and organisational models

When deciding how to organise a particular lesson or unit of work the teacher must answer seven questions:

- **What *exactly* do I want pupils to gain from this experience?**

Objectives should always be considered before activities. They should be derived from previous learning and assessment of pupil attainment. They may be defined in terms of knowledge, concepts, skills or personal qualities. If there are multiple objectives the teacher must prioritise these and select a manageable number. The objectives should be shared with the pupils at an age-appropriate level so that they are aware of the purpose of a session or unit of work.

- **How can I measure their success against these objectives?**

Not only will the teacher need to decide this; he or she will also need to make this explicit to the pupils.

- **Which type of activity best meets these objectives?**

A single approach may be appropriate or the teacher may need to mix and match.

- **Which method of organisation will create the best climate for the successful completion of these activities?**

- What will *my* role be in various parts of the session or unit?

In some settings the teacher may also need to consider the deployment of classroom assistants, students or volunteers.

- How can I accommodate pupils of varying abilities and pupils with more challenging behaviour?

- Which is the best way to organise the classroom for this session or unit?

In the following case studies two teachers consider these questions.

## Case study 8.1

### Geography at Key Stage 1

Mrs Robinson teaches a mixed class of 27 Year 1 and Year 2 pupils in a prosperous suburb. Overall, the children are making good progress against National Curriculum Attainment Targets and National Strategy Targets. Of the 18 Year 2 pupils, six are operating at least a year above their chronological age with regard to their geographical understanding. All the other Year 2 pupils operate at age-appropriate levels with the exception of two boys who are operating at Year 1 level. Three of the nine Year 1 pupils have general learning difficulties and, of these, two are non-readers. These two pupils are relatively immature, have short concentration spans and can be disruptive. Mrs Robinson has the support of a classroom assistant, Mrs Underwood, for two afternoons each week. She has a conventional rectangular classroom space with access to a shared group room and a shared 'wet area'.

It is the Summer term. Guided by the QCA Schemes of Work Mrs Robinson is planning a series of sessions to raise pupil awareness of differences between particular localities. The children in Year 2 have previously studied the immediate locality of the school but the children in Year 1 have not. Pupil records show that most of the Year 2 children could previously name and recall key features of their own environment. Some of the more able Year 1 children were able to point out and name simple features according to their Foundation stage records. The children are generally well travelled. Most have been abroad and almost all have been to a seaside town.

Mrs Robinson considers the key questions:

### What exactly do I want pupils to learn from this experience?

There are some objectives specific to Year 2 pupils, some specific to Year 1 and some more generic objectives. I have chosen the following as my priority:

### All pupils

To be able to name physical and manmade geographical features.

### Year 1 pupils

To recognise and recall key geographical features in the local suburb of Westbury:

### Year 2 pupils

To recall key geographical features in the local suburb. To compare these with geographical features in a nearby small seaside resort and note similarities and differences.

To consider why different areas have different features and amenities (more able pupils).

## How can I measure their success against these objectives?

The objectives are knowledge- and skill-based.

Pupil success will be gauged through contributions in teacher-led discussion and accurate responses with activity materials.

## Which type of activity best meets these objectives?

This is the first session in a new unit for the pupils so I will begin with direct exposition to keep the session tightly focused on the objectives. I have then planned differentiated reinforcement activities for the majority of the pupils and enrichment activities for the most able. I have decided to bring the pupils back together for direct exposition at the end of the session to reinforce the objectives and make an informal assessment of pupil learning.

## Which method of organisation will create the best climate for the completion of these activities?

The youngest and least able pupils are the ones most difficult to engage. I have decided that the three least-able Y1 pupils, together with three other model Y1 pupils, should be supported by Mrs Underwood and engage in direct exposition and reinforcement activity away from the rest of the group, rejoining the class at the conclusion of the session.

Before the lesson begins I will set out the resources needed for each group activity on the children's tables. Generic resources like scissors and glue are available in their usual places. I like the children to collect these by themselves as it develops their autonomy.

## How can I accommodate pupils of varying abilities and pupils with more challenging behaviour?

There is a wide range of ability and maturity in this mixed-age class. Because the objectives have been differentiated the tasks need to reflect this. The least able and least mature pupils will receive the highest level of support from the classroom assistant, ensuring that they remain on task and do not disrupt other pupils. The most able will be attempting an activity not directly anticipated in the whole-class session. To ensure that they understand this task and engage in challenging discussion I will work with this group. The remaining two groups should be able to work independently as their tasks are closely related to whole-class work.

## What will *my* role be in various parts of the session or unit?

Before the lesson begins I will brief Mrs Underwood about the nature of her task with her group and suggest key questions and vocabulary she might use. I will prepare sets of pictures and sorting grids for each group. These will be placed on the tables in advance. I will also prepare some activities for early finishers.

When the lesson begins I will remind children of acceptable standards of behaviour. I will introduce the theme of the work and make the objectives of the session clear. I will help the children recall key geographical features in the locality and model the correct vocabulary. I will outline group tasks and dismiss children to their tables. I will be based with Group 3, setting challenging questions, but will have an overview of the other two groups in the room. At the close of the session I will oversee tidying of the classroom and bring the children back to the carpet. I will reinforce learning through structured discussion and ensure an orderly dismissal.

After the session I will liaise with Mrs Underwood about attainment within her group. I will examine pupil work for evidence of attainment at a new level.

## What is the best way to organise the classroom for these activities?

There will need to be a large clear space for whole-group time at the beginning and end of the session. The tables should be organised to accommodate four groups. Around the edges of the room there should be space to set out activities for early finishers. The location of generic resources is already known to pupils, as is the location for completed work.

## This is an account of the lesson:

The children are asked to sit in a circle on the mat. Mrs Robinson gains their attention with a familiar hand-clapping routine. The subject matter is introduced to the whole class, briefly. Mrs Underwood's group then leaves for field work in the locality with the digital cameras. Their brief is to record key features in photographs and words with Mrs Underwood as their scribe. On their return to the classroom they work with Mrs Underwood to write captions for their photographs. They will be based in the small group room but will join the rest of the class at the end of the session.

Once this group has left Mrs Robinson begins a period of direct exposition with the whole class. She asks the pupils to close their eyes and directs them on an imaginary walk through the locality. At various points she asks the pupils to tell her what they can 'see'. She asks two of the most able pupils to list these suggestions. She then asks these pupils to read back the features pupils have named. At the end, pupils are invited to add any features that have been omitted from the list. Mrs Robinson praises the pupils and gives a brief explanation of the differentiated group activities that are to follow. The tables in the classroom are arranged so that groups of four to six pupils look inward at each other.

Group 1 – remaining Y1 pupils and less-able Y2 pupils have a selection of pictures of local features, also some features which belong in a seaside resort. Their task is first to sort these features into two groups **in Westbury** and **not in Westbury** using prepared sorting grids and gluesticks. They then label these features.

Group 2 – Y2 pupils work at an age-appropriate level and also have pictures to sort. Their task is slightly more demanding as they must sort pictures into features which you can find **in Westbury**, features **from a seaside town** and features which you find **in both**.

Group 3 – more-able Year 2 pupils. Again these pupils are provided with a set of pictures to study, this time all from a seaside locality and all human features. They are asked to think about why these features are present, particularly in a seaside location, and record their ideas in simple sentences. Collaborative discussion is encouraged as is the use of a scribe. One sentence is modelled for them. Because the task for Group 3 is the greatest departure from the whole-class exposition, Mrs Robinson decides to base herself with this group to ensure that their task is fully grasped and to deepen the discussion with appropriate closed and open questions.

Early finishers select from the following:

- a box of tourist information leaflets about both the town in which the children live and a local seaside town;

- a small-world town and road mat which has been set out on the floor in the wet area;

- some jigsaws of suburban and seaside scenes.

When the majority of children have finished their task Mrs Robinson asks them to tidy away their equipment and return to the circle with their work. Mrs Underwood also brings her group to the circle with the photograph book they have made.

Mrs Robinson reinforces the objectives of the lesson with closed questioning, inviting contributions from each of the groups. She uses pupils' names to maintain attention and models attentive body language when pupils are speaking. Mrs Underwood sits among her group, again modelling attentive behaviour and prompting pupils either to listen or to contribute as appropriate. Towards the end of the discussion Mrs Robinson introduces some more open-ended questions such as 'Why do you think there are more benches at the seaside than in Westbury?'

She completes the lesson with praise for the pupils and a promise of field work in a seaside location to deepen their understanding.

Pupils are dismissed from the room group by group. On their way out of the room they leave their work in the 'finished work' box.

## Case study 8.2

### Art at Key Stage 2

Mr Lockwood teaches a class of 24 Y6 pupils on a large, local authority housing estate in a big city. There is a significant minority of pupils with special needs in the class. English is the second language for nine children in the class, although they can communicate in English. One of these pupils is supported for three afternoons by an E2L assistant.

Pupil records and informal observations by Mr Lockwood show that pupils respond enthusiastically to art activities but are less confident when analysing their own work and that of others. It is the Summer term and Mr Lockwood is ready to tackle the QCA unit on ***People in Action***.

Mr Lockwood considers the key questions:

**What exactly do I want pupils to gain from this experience?**

Pupils to look more analytically at art work.

Pupils to express views more fully and with greater fluency.

Pupils to listen more carefully to others.

Pupils to explore some simple drawing techniques to show movement.

**How can I measure their success against these objectives?**

Through the quality of their contributions in pair and whole-class discussion.

Through their initial attempts at drawing techniques.

**Which type of activity best meets these objectives?**

Some exposition to clarify objectives and key vocabulary; also to demonstrate specific skills.

Some reinforcement activities to develop speaking and listening skills.

Some reinforcement/enrichment activities to develop drawing technique. These may be differentiated.

**How can I accommodate pupils of varying abilities and pupils with more challenging behaviour?**

The E2L classroom assistant will work constantly with the four children who are least confident in their use of English.

Pairing of children may be directed to avoid unproductive or disruptive liaisons.

**Which method of organisation will create the best climate for the successful completion of these activities?**

Whole-class and collaborative pair work for development of discussion skills. The pairs can be random or friendship groups.

Whole-class and individual work for the development of drawing skills.

**What will my role be in various parts of the session or unit?**

To lead whole-class and pair discussion to develop analytical responses.

To monitor paired discussion.

To demonstrate particular drawing techniques.

**Which is the best way to organise the classroom for this session or unit?**

Desks need to be arranged in a horseshoe formation facing a central whiteboard. This means that all pupils can see demonstrations of drawing techniques but can also engage in discussion with a neighbour.

This is an account of the lesson:

Mr Lockwood introduces the theme of comic book action. He asks each pupil to browse through the comic book in front of them to find images of people or animals in motion, then look closely at how that movement is portrayed. After ten minutes of individual study Mr Lockwood divides the pupils into pairs. He asks them to describe their favourite technique to their partner. He warns them in advance that they will be describing their partner's preferred technique so it is very important that they listen carefully. After a further ten minutes Mr Lockwood calls the pupils back together. He then asks for pupils to report back. In this feedback session Mr Lockwood demonstrates particular drawing techniques. He also invites some pupils to demonstrate techniques they have seen.

Less-able pupils are then given samples of images on individual cards. Their task is to make an accurate copy of these in their sketchbooks. More-able pupils are asked to create a sketch of themselves running, using one of the drawing techniques used in the comic books. Early finishers may attempt a new image or a new technique.

Mr Lockwood draws the class together and summarises the techniques seen. He takes a vote on the favourite technique.

## Conclusion

In conclusion, then, a teacher needs to know *why* they are teaching a particular lesson. If they are clear in this respect then the *how, when* and *where* should follow.

## Suggestions for further reading

Alexander, R. (2000) *Culture and Pedagogy: International Comparisons in Primary Education*. Oxford: Blackwell.

If you never read another research book, make sure you read this one. Robin Alexander has compared primary education across five countries. Part 4: Classrooms compares the different organisations within classrooms and their effects on learning.

## References

Alexander, R.J., Rose, J. and Woodhead, C. (1992) *Classroom Organisation and Classroom Practice in Primary Schools*. London: Department for Education and Science.

Bennett, N. (1976) *Teaching Styles and Pupil Progress*. Cambridge, MA: Harvard University Press.

Bennett, N., Desforges, C., Cockburn, A. and Wilkinson, B. (1984) *The Quality of Pupil Learning Experiences*. London: Routledge.

Department for Education and Employment (1998) *The National Literacy Strategy: A Framework for Teaching*. London: DfEE.

Department for Education and Employment (1999) *The National Numeracy Strategy: A Framework for Teaching*. London: DfEE.

Department for Education and Science (1988) *The Education Reform Act*. London: HMSO.

Edwards, C.H. (2004) *Classroom Discipline and Management* (4th edn). Hobeken: Wiley Jossey-Bass Education.

Kyriacou, C. (2001) *Effective Teaching in Schools: Theory and Practice*. Cheltenham: Nelson Thornes.

Plowden Report (1967) *Children and their Primary Schools*. London: HMSO.

Qualifications and Curriculum Authority (2000) *Schemes of Work at Key Stages 1 and 2*. London: QCA.

Smith, R.G. and Coldron, J. (1999) 'Conditions for Learning as a Teacher'. *Journal of In-service Eduction*, **25**(2), 245–60.

Whitaker, P. (1995) *Managing to Learn: Aspects of Reflective and Experiential Learning in Schools*. London: Cassell.

Yapp, N. (1987) *Bluff Your Way in Teaching*. Horsham: Ravette Books.

# The individual in the primary classroom

Lynn Newton

# 9

## Introduction

The fundamental task of any teacher is to help all the pupils in his or her class to learn. In other words, your main role is to support all pupils in the process of achieving their learning potential. These two processes – teaching and learning – are distinct yet clearly interrelated, although the relationship is far from simple. In discussing education for all, Blair (2002) tells us:

> Technical competencies in teaching are important but not sufficient in a diverse, class-based, gendered, multi-ethnic, multi-faith, multilingual society. Teachers now need to think in more complex multi-dimensional ways in order to promote a culture of inclusiveness in the classroom and the school as a whole. (Blair 2002: 12)

This is not an easy task for any teacher but it can be done.

Children are learning all the time, with or without you as their teacher to support the process. They are constantly trying to make sense of the world around them and their experiences in that world, whether they are at home or at school. Consequently, each child in your class is unique as a learner; they come to you with different abilities and levels of development, varied prior experiences, personal needs and interests, and their own developing learning styles. As their teacher, you will need first to get to know them as individuals so that you can match the learning experiences you offer to what you judge to be appropriate to their needs, abilities and interests, all within the framework of a curriculum probably based on the National Curriculum Orders. This is sometimes described as matching. This, as most teachers will tell you, is not an easy thing to do. Given that every child is different, you could, potentially, be trying to design 30-plus different sets of lessons for each teaching day – an impossible task. That degree of realism is necessary is clear when we consider the infinite range of interactions possible in your classroom between the three fundamental components: (1) you as teacher; (2) your pupils as learners; and (3) the curriculum requirements you must meet. This relationship is summarised in Figure 9.1.

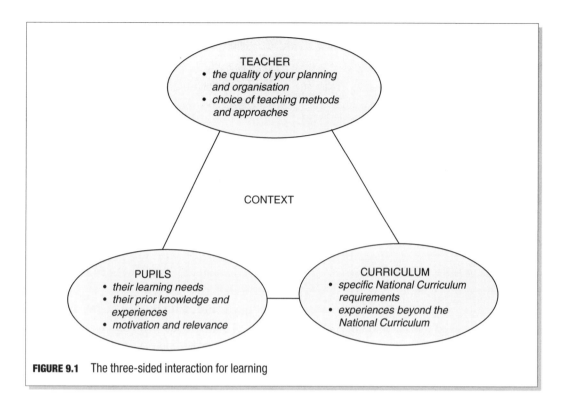

**FIGURE 9.1**   The three-sided interaction for learning

Every one of these interactions might reasonably be expected to contribute to the progress your pupils make in their learning. Add to this picture the context in which you and they are working and you will appreciate why realism is necessary.

You will need to keep the notion of quality learning experiences in mind when planning your lessons. A learning experience of high quality should do several things. It should:

■ consolidate the development of skills, the acquisition of knowledge or the construction of understanding;

■ enable the pupils to take the next step in their learning;

■ result in learning that can be used and applied in new contexts;

■ be a coherent part of the learning process, contributing to and supporting other learning activities across the curriculum;

■ be seen by the pupils as being relevant to their development and is thus motivating; and

■ be differentiated to match the assessed needs of the pupils as part of the progressive development of their skills, knowledge and understanding.

To do this, you will need to think particularly about the individual needs of the children and the differences between them.

## Activity 9.1

When in school, ask the class teacher to identify three children whom he or she knows to be different as learners. Track the three children for a day and see how they behave as learners in different contexts, including social contexts, e.g. break times. Keep notes and discuss your observations with your teacher at the end of the day.

In this chapter, we will look in particular at the idea of an education for all children. In particular, the concepts of equal opportunity and differentiation will be discussed.

## What? Starting with the curriculum

The origin of the word curriculum is the Latin *currere* meaning 'the course to be run' and, historically, schools have established content area courses (curricula) through which pupils progress, often culminating in tests or examinations. Today, the term curriculum is used in education in a variety of ways. It can be used in a very broad and general way, to encompass everything your school does. It can also be used in a very narrow and specific way to describe an educational activity designed for an individual child at a particular time in a particular area. Since children differ in their social, emotional, cultural and intellectual backgrounds; prior experiences; and aptitudes and interests, what they actually learn will inevitably be different to, and wider than, what teachers intend to teach through the curriculum experiences offered.

Whilst planning is important, what is equally important is the quality of those experiences, the context in which they are offered and the extent to which you cater for their individual needs and preferences. Some pupils prefer to work alone; others with peers. Some prefer peace and quiet; others are used to background noise and find silence uncomfortable. Some prefer to read while seated; others prefer to lie on the floor. No single learning style is best, although as a teacher you may feel that some are more appropriate in particular contexts than others. Primary pupils are still developing their learning styles and you can support them by varying the opportunities you provide for them, but always with the overall effectiveness of your teaching in mind.

## Who? The case for equal opportunities

Those awarded Qualified Teacher Status must value diversity and have high expectations of all their pupils. The Standards (TTA 2003) are very specific about this. You need to show that you have high expectations of all pupils and understand how your pupils' learning can be affected by their physical, intellectual, linguistic, social, cultural and emotional development. You will need to take account of and support your pupils' varying needs when planning lessons, and set challenging teaching and learning objectives that are relevant to all pupils in your classes, taking account of varying backgrounds. In other words, you must respond effectively to equal opportunities issues.

Equality of educational opportunity does not simply mean treating all pupils the same. By doing that, you are not necessarily recognising and valuing their difference and uniqueness. The Education Reform Act (DES 1988) provides a framework for equal opportunities within which teachers must work. The focus should be on needs, opportunities, expectations and potential, and your school will have developed a policy for equal opportunity practices.

In discussing Standard S1.1 – *Having high expectations of all pupils* – the TTA guidance (2003) advocates:

> All children and young people are entitled to an education that develops their potential and widens their opportunities. Teachers are expected to have a professional commitment to raising the educational achievement of all their pupils, whatever their background or current level of achievement. (TTA 2003: 6)

Consequently, you will need to plan and teach so that every child in your class has the opportunity to access the experiences and make progress in line with his or her potential, regardless of sex, race or ability. This criterion underpins *Meeting pupils' needs* (Standard S3.2.4):

> Those awarded Qualified Teacher Status must demonstrate that they identify and support more able pupils, those who are working below age-related expectations, those who are failing to achieve their potential in learning, and those who experience behavioural, emotional and social difficulties. (TTA 2003: 35)

Generally, while catering for the needs of all the pupils in your class, there are some groups of children who need particular attention. You need to think about their age, cultural backgrounds, gender, the gifted and talented pupils and those with special educational needs. The important areas of special educational needs and gifted and talented learners will be discussed in Chapter 10.

## Age and ability

Not only are there physical variations in what the children are able to do at different ages but also the variety of learning needs in terms of intellectual ability can be large. The Cockcroft Report (DES 1982) referred to the seven-year spread of ability in any primary classroom. In terms of mathematics ability, in a Y4 class of 8–9 year-olds (KS2) there could be some pupils working at the level of 5–6-year-olds (Y1, KS1) and others working at the level of 11–12-year-olds (Y7, KS3). The National Curriculum levels reflect such a spread of ability within an age group, to be taken into account when you plan and assess. In addition, you may well find yourself in a class with a mixed-age group. A small rural school could have Y3 to Y6 (7+ to 10+ years) all together in one class. This could mean that you could potentially have children who are working at the level of a Reception class child alongside one who is working at the level of a secondary Year 9 student (13–14-year-old)! Differentiation is crucial in such a situation.

## Cultural background

The cultural background of pupils can influence their learning in a variety of ways. As a starting point, ask yourself questions about your own perceptions of the home experiences of working-class or ethnic minority children. There seems to be a direct relationship between culture and learning style.

By recognising and valuing cultural diversity, you will be able to create a meaningful and purposeful learning environment for all pupils. Think about the extent to which the home environment and cultural traditions of these pupils might influence the following:

■ What are the *language opportunities* for the pupil? What is the language spoken at home? To what extent is English an additional language only used in the school context? Are the pupils encouraged to be assertive or to speak out about things? Is the oral tradition viewed as more important than the written one?

■ Is *non-verbal communication* a significant factor? Are certain gestures disapproved of? Is eye contact with adults allowed? What are considered 'good manners'? Are there any influential customs or behaviours to be considered?

■ What *other factors* might be culturally determined? Is time of day important? Are there routines that may be relevant? Are there aspects of clothing, food or lifestyle that can be used positively as a stimulus for learning?

## Gender

That boys and girls are different is obvious. That they may be different as learners is less obvious. Yet any teacher will tell you that this is the case. There is copious research on gender issues in primary education. Links between girls and underachievement in science, and boys and underperformance in the arts, are well documented. Inadvertently, discrimination against both boys and girls can occur in primary classrooms. The nature of the tasks and activities, the gender representation in books and other audio-visual resources, the use of praise and reward, the use of questions – all these can have a gender bias inadvertently built into them. For example, think about:

■ Are boys given more behavioural attention and direct instruction than girls?

■ Do pictures in books and charts show girls *and* boys, and are different races and cultures represented?

■ Are activities offered to both girls *and* boys, for example, playing with construction kits or doing some needlework?

■ Who receives the most attention in mathematics lessons or in reading time?

Race and gender issues have implications for how you organise your classroom groups. There may be cultural differences about gender interaction, personal space and eye contact which will emerge in discussion that you may need to think about. It is important to remember that these are particular situations to watch for in your classroom, but all children have the same rights to access learning. It really should be education for all.

---

## Activity 9.2

Does the teacher seem to plan with equal opportunity in mind?
Are there any incidents where children are not being treated in line with the policy statement on equal opportunity?

---

## How? The case for differentiation

Teachers will tell you that they have taught the same age group for 10 years but no two classes have been the same. Children are different. To cater for these different needs and abilities you will have to *differentiate* in some way. In essence, the intellectual and practical demands made should be suited to the abilities of all pupils, allowing the highest possible standards to be achieved by the most able pupils, while catering for the needs of those pupils unable to reach those standards. At the same time it should provide the essential experience of a broad and balanced programme for all pupils. So how can you do this?

Differentiation can mean different things to different people. For this reason, it can be difficult to define. A useful explanation of the concept of differentiation is provided by Blake and Hanley (1995: 50):

> Learners differ in their needs, aptitudes and capabilities and differentiation is an acknowledgement of the differences. As far as learning and teaching are concerned, the term is best explained as the process of matching learning tasks to particular groups or individuals. Teachers, therefore, have to consider differences when planning and teaching lessons in order to ensure that all abilities in the class are catered for. The approach can be based on differentiation by task or by outcome.

In essence, the intellectual and practical demands made of your pupils should be suited to their abilities. Hence the earlier mention of the concept of *match*. Their prior experiences and abilities should be taken into account when planning new experiences.

In the extreme, differentiation can result in a totally separate education for some children (as with Special Schools or Special Units within a mainstream context). Occasionally, it can mean a separate programme for some children for part or all of the time (an Individual Education Plan or IEP). More commonly, it can involve streaming or grouping by ability within a class. As a teacher, differentiation is a process you use to help the pupils in your class tackle their work at their own level of ability. By differentiating, you support them individually to achieve appropriate skills, knowledge or understanding targets as identified by the National Curriculum requirements for assessment.

Once teachers have got to know their class, and drawing on information in records maintained by the previous teachers, they often sort the children into groups. The groups can be based on friendship, gender or ability. Sometimes the groupings can vary across subjects. An extreme, but real-life, example is a school where teachers use one set of groups based on ability for English, another based on ability for mathematics, a third based on gender for science, and groups based on friendship for the other curricular activities. In schools with more than one class of pupils per year group, streaming by ability is becoming more common.

The process of differentiation is further complicated by the fact that almost everything you do with your class can be differentiated. For example, consider differentiation of:

assessment and testing

classroom organisation and management

cognitive demand of the tasks and activities

expectations

grouping of children

interests / motivations of pupils

language used (spoken and written)

pupils' preferred learning styles

questioning strategies

resources used

tasks and activities

teacher / teaching assistant support

teaching styles

timing and pacing.

The list could go on and it is deliberately in alphabetical order to emphasise that no one approach, strategy or technique is more appropriate or useful than any other. However, it is useful for planning to think about differentiating by:

- content – provide different tasks/activities for different pupils;

- outcome – have different expectations from the same task/activity;

- support – provide verbal or written support for some pupils and not others;

- resources – limit or structure the resources used by some pupils;

- language – adjust your vocabulary to suit different groups;

- group – have the pupils in groups by ability, each with specific targets;

- worksheet – have different work cards / task sheets for different pupils;

- time – allow less able pupils longer to complete tasks.

Such a list makes it sound very straightforward. In reality, differentiation is as difficult to organise as it is to define. In an ideal world differentiation would be at the level of the individual child. So in a class of 35 pupils you would have 35 separate (differentiated) programmes running. In the *real* world, you are unlikely to have the time, the resources or the energy to operate such a system. Most teachers operate the class as three, four or five differentiated groups.

There is no single, simple model for differentiation. One possible way of working, used by many teachers, is shown in Figure 9.2. The model begins with the medium-term planning in that it focuses on the learning experiences that are central to the teaching of the whole class. This is the 'core' – the skills to be developed, knowledge acquired and understanding constructed as a result of the learning experience. In your preliminary planning, you will need to identify the targets and outcomes for the lesson. Within this you will need to identify the skills, knowledge and understanding that are to be introduced in some way to the whole class. To do this you need to make judgements about starting points and prior experiences, drawing on assessment evidence. You will then need to identify the main route in terms of the breadth of the experiences, pacing and timing, the language you are using to question and explain and the resources you will require.

At this point you should begin to see that more than one route will be needed. Some pupils will need support in some way – by you, by a classroom assistant, through hint or cue cards, by a tape recording of instructions etc. These may be pupils who are less able or have some sort of learning or physical disability. It may be that you must consider the needs of more able children. This suggests that you will need to think about at least two groups, one either side of the main route. Your next step then will be to identify two further levels of activity and experience, making three in total. In reality, this number should be a reflection of the needs and diversity of the children in your class. The experiences you select for the different groups should have at their heart the core skills, knowledge and understanding identified earlier. They will, however, be varied in terms of breadth and depth of content, pace and timing, support and reinforcement, enrichment and language used. However, remember that the more groups you have the harder it is to plan, organise, monitor and assess the different groups.

Less-able pupils will, in general, need sharply focused experiences, broken down into small stages or steps, perhaps involving simplified or supported language and located in concrete, relevant contexts. This will enable reinforcement of the learning experiences. On the other hand, more able pupils can usually be given deeper and more open-ended tasks in which they take more responsibility themselves for the pacing and timing of the

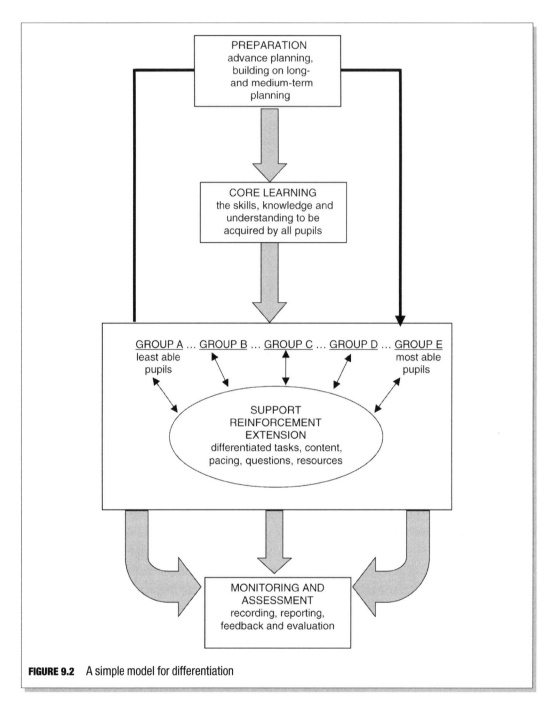

**FIGURE 9.2**  A simple model for differentiation

experiences and locating the relevant contexts. They also enjoy using extended and specialist vocabulary.

The final stage would be a plenary session, in which the different groups gather together to discuss their experiences. During this process you would interact with the pupils in different ways and for different purposes, including monitoring progress and collecting assessment evidence.

A simple model like this has certain weaknesses. It works on the basis of an average group. It assumes that most teachers identify the children in their class who are in the middle of the spread of ability and one or two groups of children either side of these. This, of course, leads to difficulties in how you define and measure the different needs and abilities and how you select for the different groups. For example, as already mentioned, all learners can benefit from extension and reinforcement activities, depending upon the nature of the experience. A way to deal with this is to start with an open-ended activity for all the children, in order to find out where the children are. Then design a set of National Curriculum-related experiences at several different levels to locate the individuals within the class. Adjust the groups so that the children are matched. However, evaluate children's progress regularly and be willing to change the groups so that the children are not fixed in one group.

## Conclusion

When planning for differentiation, you need to think about how information and activities are presented to your pupils. Some general rules might include:

- plan carefully what new skills, knowledge and understanding need to be presented to all your pupils;
- identify what prior knowledge or experiences your pupils have already had and should have in order to acquire new skills, knowledge or understanding;
- select the most appropriate and relevant way of introducing the new information to set the scene, capture attention and motivate the pupils;
- plan for focused questioning by identifying the key questions and the cognitive purposes they serve;
- consider alternative strategies that support understanding, such as the use of a practical activity or an analogy;
- plan appropriate reinforcement and extension activities to support the new information being presented in different ways;
- keep oral and written instructions or directions simple, so encouraging pupils' independence on task and avoiding information overload;
- present instructions for non-readers in alternative ways, such as through pictures or tape-recorded directions;
- communicate written tasks in an attractive and appealing way, using short sentences, simple vocabulary and illustrations;
- ensure that all pupils are familiar with the key vocabulary by using wordlists, dictionaries, labelled diagrams or similar forms of support;

- allow mixed-ability groups so that there can be peer support;

- use other adults, school auxiliaries, teaching assistants and parents (such adults will need precise instructions); and

- have expectations appropriate to the pupils' needs, interests and abilities and recognise all pupils' successes.

Planning for differentiated learning therefore involves more than simply planning what set of learning experiences should be offered to children in your class. It requires identifying the knowledge, skills, concepts and attitudes children should understand or develop. This means you will need to be aware of how children learn generally, how they learn within subject disciplines, what other experiences they have had and what your role or function will be in encouraging that learning. One of the most thorough research studies of classroom tasks is that of Desforges (1985). He has shown that there are four main types of task that you can consider when planning a range of learning experiences:

- incremental tasks to introduce new skills or ideas;

- restructuring tasks which require the child to invent or discover an idea;

- enrichment tasks that involve the child in applying familiar skills or ideas to new problems or situations; and

- practice tasks that encourage the use of new skills in familiar problems or situations.

All pupils benefit from experience of this range of tasks at various times. If there is space in your classroom, a system that lends itself well to supporting individual learning experiences is the *learning centre* or *learning station*. A learning station provides opportunities for reinforcement and enrichment of a topic or theme. It enables pupils to work independently or with a friend to explore experiences, ideas of interest and new challenges. Learning stations have the added advantage that they also allow you to provide and control access to resources and materials.

It is erroneous to think that, for example, more-able children only need enrichment and less-able ones practice tasks. The rules are:

- find out about all the pupils in your class and use that information positively;

- use evidence of past achievement to set challenging learning objectives and individual targets;

- select resources in a way that shows that diversity is valued and sensitivity to the needs of different groups;

- show a commitment to enabling pupils from all backgrounds to make progress in learning; and

- show an awareness of the different approaches that various pupils take to their work and of their developing organisational and cognitive skills.

If you can show evidence of doing these, then you will be recognising and valuing difference and helping all your pupils achieve their potential.

## Activity 9.3

When you are in school, ask your teacher to identify a child in your class whom you can observe in detail across a range of lessons and activities. As you observe the child, make notes on what he/she does. Focus in particular on:

- the general level of interest shown by the child in each lesson;
- how the child participated in each lesson in terms of asking and answering questions, interacting with other children and contributing to the lesson;
- how often the child was on task and off task;
- the quality of the child's written work;
- how the child behaved when he/she encountered difficulties;
- how independent the child was, and
- how the teacher responded to the child's needs.

What do your notes tell you about the child's needs? What strategies for differentiation to meet these needs can you use to help this child? Discuss your ideas with the class teacher.

## Case study 9.1: Alan

I teach Year 3 (7–8-year-olds) in a first school in the north of England. I've been teaching for over 12 years and I'm the curriculum leader for humanities in my school; that's history, geography and RE. I try to differentiate most of the lessons I plan, but sometimes it's more effective than others.

For me, the essence of differentiation is that all the pupils in my class can access the content on offer. This means I have to think about different strategies and approaches and different techniques for teaching and learning. You see, there's no single right way to teach, just as there's no single way all children learn. That means when you think of all the things that you can do and that pupils can do, you can differentiate almost anything.

For example, we were doing the topic of the Vikings in history. I'd done the pre-course planning during half-term. This meant that I knew what my overall aims and objectives were. I'd worked out the general content for the seven lessons – there was one a week for the whole of the half-term up to Easter. For each lesson, this started with the skills that I wanted the children to use and the ideas I wanted them all to come away with from the topic (the core skills, knowledge and understanding). In the lesson on travel and ships, I wanted them all to learn the word 'longboat' and know what a longboat looked like. For most children this is straightforward, but for one or two this is a challenge; they have difficulty learning the word 'cat'!

The next thing I do is think about how the groups can be supported and challenged. I have four groups in my class working at three levels. There is a small group of five more-able pupils. Two groups of six are the middle-of-the-roaders. Finally, there's a group of seven less able. I take the activities I am going to do with the two middle groups as the starting point – all the class will do these. I use a TV programme on video showing Vikings making and using a longboat. We all watch it. There's some reading to do, a worksheet of questions and a card longboat to cut out and build. The reading is supported for the less-able group by using headphones and a tape recorder. They listen and read. The question sheet is also slightly different. There are fewer questions and I do some hint cards (words, spellings, pictures and so on). For the more able, there's some extra reading connected with travel and routes – links to geography really. There's also a computer program they can use to find out more to answer the questions.

When they've all finished we all get together and create a Viking harbour with the card models they've made. I have a question-and-answer game to finish, with questions pitched at different levels so that I can target individuals. This partly allows me to assess their learning, alongside their written work and contributions to the discussion. I make notes of what they do and say in order to build a picture of their learning.

Here are some tips. Start the first lesson with an open-ended activity to help you find out where the children are. This can be tied in to the National Curriculum level appropriate for the whole class and will allow you to see what they know and can do. Change the groups so that the children aren't in the same group for all subjects and all topics. They won't become stereotyped. Also, evaluate regularly so you know where the children have got to as individuals – their rate of progress isn't always the same.

## Suggestions for further reading

If you would like to explore some of the issues touched upon in this chapter, the following books should be of interest to you:

Blair, M. (2002), 'Education for all', in M. Cole (ed.), *Professional Values and Practice for Teachers and Student Teachers* (2nd edn). London: David Fulton Publishers, Chapter 1, pp. 1–15.

Blair's chapter provides an excellent introduction to the notion of education for all and provides the context for exploring the issues of diversity and multiculturalism.

Hughes, P. (2002) *Principles of Primary Education Study Guide* (2nd edn). London: David Fulton Publishers.

The study guide provides practical guidance on issues and legislative frameworks that underpin professional practice. Of particular relevance to differentiation is Chapter 2, 'Children's learning', pp. 7–13.

Suschitzky, W. (1995) 'It's not fair! Equal opportunities in practice', in J. Moyles (ed.) *Beginning Teaching: Beginning Learning In Primary Education*. Buckingham: Open University Press, Chapter 13, pp. 217–30.

This chapter provides a useful overview of the complex issues underpinning the equal opportunities debate in primary education. There is also a comprehensive list of references which could take you further.

## References

Blair, M. (2002) 'Education for all', in M. Cole, (ed.), *Professional Values and Practice for Teachers and Student Teachers* (2nd edn). London: David Fulton Publishers, Chapter 1, pp. 1–15.

Blake, D. and Hanley, V. (1995) *The Dictionary of Educational Terms*. Aldershot: Arena.

Department of Education and Science (DES) (1988) *The Education Reform Act*. London: HMSO.

Desforges, C. (1985) 'Matching tasks to children', in N. Bennett and C. Desforges (eds) *Recent Advances in Classroom Research*. Edinburgh: Scottish Academic Press.

Teacher Training Agency (TTA) (2003) *Qualifying to Teach: Handbook of Guidance*. London: TTA.

# Different needs and different responses

## Tracey Hume

## Introduction

If the child does not learn in the way in which we teach, then we must teach him in the way in which he learns. (Pollock and Waller 1994: 176)

The above quotation summarises well a good teacher's attitude to children with different needs and will form the main thrust of this chapter.

As a trainee or newly qualified teacher you may well hope that it will be some years before you have to face the difficulties and challenges of teaching many children with different needs, but unfortunately this will not be the case. Different needs are found in every classroom and every school; they are not confined to special schools. The Code of Practice for Special Educational Needs (DfES 2001) makes it very clear that 'All teachers are teachers of children with special educational needs' (5.2). The following may help put it into perspective.

### The scale of the problem

In a class of 30 children you may have:

- three children with dyslexia – approximately 10 per cent of the population have some degree of this specific learning difficulty. (Taken from approximate figures by the British Dyslexia Association, 1996.);

- three children may be on the Gifted and Talented register – the DfES recommends a 10 per cent cohort from each year group;

- one child with an Autistic Spectrum or Language Disorder; one child in 86 is said to be on the autistic spectrum;

- two children with Attention Deficit and Hyperactivity Disorder (ADHD); approximately 5 per cent of the school-aged population suffers with ADHD;

- up to three children with some degree of dyspraxia; it has been determined that up to 10 per cent of the population have some degree of dyspraxia (co-ordination and motor difficulties) according to the National Institute of Mental Health;

- two children who have English as a second language; in 2002 it was estimated that 7.5 per cent of school-aged children do not have English as their first language;

- up to six children may have some difficulty with their sight; this is according to figures produced by the RNIB, in 1991;

- one child may have an emotional and/or behavioural disorder (EBD); there are no clear figures for EBD but most teachers would say they had at least one in every class; and

- as many as four children may have some hearing loss; according to the UK council on deafness, 15 per cent of the population experience some hearing loss ranging from mild to profound deafness.

Out of the class of 30 children, this could leave as few as five children with apparently no obvious difficulties or differences. Clearly, there is no such thing as an 'average' class, and this fictitious class is an extreme example and is unlikely to exist. It is also possible, of course, that one child may have two or more of these difficulties which would reduce the number of actual children with differences. In recent years there has been an apparent increase in the prevalence of many disorders including autism and specific learning difficulties such as dyslexia and dyspraxia. If such trends continue the number of children with different needs is likely to increase in the future. Thus, during your teaching career you are more likely to encounter such pupils, and therefore it is better to be forewarned and forearmed. Different needs will quite possibly be the majority in your class and not the often-perceived minority. Every class is a mixture of needs, gifts and personalities; no two classes will be the same. In order to help each child all teachers must equip themselves with a range of techniques, resources and knowledge to enable them to help each child access the curriculum and achieve their full potential.

## Activity 10.1

While in school, talk with your class teacher about the range of needs in his or her classroom. Draw up a list of the different kinds of needs that your teacher manages on a day-to-day basis. Look up needs you have not come across before.

For some teachers, a change of mindset is required. Although some different needs are due to specific physiological, neurological or emotional causes, many difficulties may be imposed by the teacher because of inflexibility of approach and restricted use of different learning styles. For most, if not all, there is a way of learning; it is up to the teacher to determine what it is and to ensure their teaching reflects it and allows the child the greatest opportunity to achieve his/her potential.

> Difficulties in learning often arise from an unsuitable environment – inappropriate grouping of pupils, inflexible teaching styles, or inaccessible curriculum materials – as much as from individual children's physical, sensory or cognitive impairments. (DfES, *Removing Barriers to Achievement*, 2004)

The example of the fictitious 'average' class may have seemed a little overwhelming. For example, it may have contained difficulties you have never encountered and seemed like a nightmare scenario. However, there are many strategies that can easily be put into place that will assist and support many of these differences at the same time, and these will be outlined later in the chapter. In addition, there are general principles for supporting children with such a wide range of differences which will enable you to teach effectively and reduce the anxiety for both you and the children. Again these will be outlined in more detail later.

## What are different needs?

The phrase 'different needs' covers a multitude of possibilities in a classroom. The main groups of needs will each be described briefly.

### Special needs and learning difficulties

> A child has special educational needs if he or she has a learning difficulty which calls for special educational provision to be made for him or her. (DfEE 1996: 7)

We are all different; we all have different needs, and for most of us these can be managed and supported in the classroom without any specific measures being put in place. We adapt our own learning methods, have various strategies which we can use, do some additional reading/research, ask parents for help or seek clarification. Children with different needs, whether they are children with special educational needs or the more gifted children, can also use these methods. However, for these children to achieve their potential more specific measures are required in the teaching and everyday support. This is especially the case with special needs; it may not always be possible for these children either to adapt their own learning style or do additional reading, as there may be inherent difficulties with cognitive understanding and/or reading. They require other people to present information in a way which suits their preferred way of learning and provide them with additional strategies to enable them to manage their own learning and access the whole curriculum.

In the 2001 Code of Practice children with learning difficulties were defined as children who have 'significantly greater difficulty in learning than the majority of children the same age' or who have a 'disability which either prevents or hinders them from making use of educational facilities of a kind generally provided for children of the same age in schools' (1.3). However, definitions are only guidelines, and barriers to learning are many and varied; while some are easily defined others are much harder to isolate, and many children with specific learning difficulties such as dyslexia, dyspraxia, ADHD or autistic spectrum disorders (ASD) can have more than one of these barriers. There is a high incidence of children with overlapping difficulties; for example, you may have a child with an autistic spectrum disorder *and* dyspraxia.

Learning difficulties can be defined in six specific areas but with an acknowledgement that many children demonstrate difficulties in more than one area:

**1**  sensory/motor difficulties – these may include hearing and sight impairments and also sensory issues relating to autistic spectrum disorders;

**2**  social/emotional difficulties – these are particularly prevalent in children with autistic spectrum disorders where a child's ability to socialise effectively and understand social cues are quite severely impaired;

**3**  physical difficulties – these may include physical disabilities, difficulties with movement around school and medical problems;

**4**  behavioural difficulties – these may include mild attention-seeking problems through to major physical disruption;

**5**  cognitive difficulties – difficulties with understanding concepts/general learning;

**6**  speech and language difficulties – these may include specific speech impairments and delay and difficulties with understanding specific aspects of language in children with autistic spectrum disorders.

## Activity 10.2

While you are in school, try to obtain a copy of the school's policy for special educational needs. Arrange a short meeting with the SEN co-ordinator (SENCO) to discuss the school's SEN policy. Use the six areas above to guide your discussion about how the policy is translated into practice.

## Gifted and talented pupils

In this country formal provision for the gifted and talented is relatively new, although this has been made informally by good teachers who have always provided differentiated experiences for all of their pupils at both ends of the learning spectrum. Awareness of, and provision for, pupils who are considered to be gifted or talented is now an important aspect of classroom planning, delivery and assessment. However, defining gifted and talented has proved quite difficult. Recently, most schools have used the definition provided in the *Excellence in Cities* documentation published in 1999 by the

DfES. This definition states that 'the gifted are those with high ability in one or more academic subject, and the talented are those with high ability in sport, music, visual arts and/or performing arts'. Schools are encouraged to identify up to 10 per cent of each year group as gifted and talented. This is achieved in a variety of ways through statutory assessment test results, staff consensus, pupil interest, achievement questionnaires, and additional tests in areas such as music, in order to identify children with natural talent who may not previously have been given opportunities to demonstrate their ability.

It is important to note that children on the gifted and talented register in each year group cohort may also be on the special needs register. Their needs do not preclude them from achieving well in a specific subject or area such as music and the performing arts. It is claimed that many people with specific learning difficulties such as dyslexia are, in fact, of above-average intelligence but their abilities have been masked by their inability to put things on paper. Children on the autistic spectrum, especially those with Asperger's syndrome or high-functioning autism, can also be of above-average intelligence. They do tend to be very good at areas such as science, computers and maths. These children often enjoy learning facts and reading a great deal of non-fiction material such as science books and can demonstrate knowledge and understanding of subjects such as space way beyond the expectations of an average primary-aged child. My own son, who has Asperger's syndrome, is typical of many in that he has great difficulty maintaining concentration during lessons and can often be seen to be 'in his own world', not listening. He can barely get a sentence written in an hour at times but can achieve level 3s across the board in Year 2 SATs, to the amazement of his teachers. These children's abilities and knowledge can be masked by their lack of social understanding and concentration difficulties.

## Specific strategies for working with gifted and talented pupils

There are some general opportunities for supporting and encouraging pupils who are gifted and some of these are outlined below but can also be found on government standards sites. Further on, I will outline some more specific ways of developing their skills and enhancing their learning.

- Group work – it is useful if children in particular subjects who are achieving well are grouped together for certain tasks in order that they can work with others of a similar ability. If there are no other children of a similar ability then a child could be grouped with children higher up the school for some lessons or educational opportunities.

- Study support/extra-curricular opportunities – in schools which have been given a good amount of additional funding for providing for gifted and talented pupils, additional activities/clubs have been provided which take place before or after school and at lunchtimes. Sometimes these are provided by teaching staff; some are provided by specialists in a particular field. The activities are not generally those which would be taught in an older class but add depth to existing work, and due to the flexibility allowed during such sessions the children can spend more time completing challenges which require them to think for themselves or to develop particular areas of interest. There is also a national scheme of summer schools for gifted and talented primary school pupils where they are taught in a secondary school using the facilities by university students or primary and secondary teachers.

■ Cluster group activities – in some areas of the country there have been successful attempts at working together with other local primary schools so that children who are gifted or talented in specific areas can take part in activities with similarly aged children from other schools.

■ Challenging resources – with children with learning difficulties we provide activities which aim to develop their understanding at the more basic end. With children on the gifted and talented register similar activities need to be provided to extend their learning and understanding beyond that expected of similarly aged children.

■ Enrichment activities – enrichment offers breadth to the gifted child's curriculum. Instead of trying to constantly push them forward in their subject area they could be given opportunities to learn new skills or take existing learning and apply it in new situations.

■ Acceleration – this is where gifted children can join an older class regularly for certain subjects in order for them to work at a level more suited to their ability and to access suitable resources. There are many issues surrounding this strategy and many schools are reluctant to choose this way forward. For example, the child may be academically ready to work at such levels but may not have the maturity, either socially or emotionally, to work with these older pupils. It can also lead to difficulties with bullying among the child's peers.

■ Homework – this is a good opportunity for the child to be given worksheets or challenges which extend their knowledge and understanding but do not make the child stand out among their peers.

■ Subject co-ordinators – you are not and cannot be an expert on everything, and while co-ordinators would not suggest that they were experts they do have access to a great deal of further information in their subject area and will receive regular mailings concerning their subject. Therefore, make sure you tap into this knowledge and information and be prepared to ask for advice.

Further information on these points can be found on the government website www.teachernet.gov.uk/teachinginengland/

## Some examples of supporting gifted and talented learners

1   During a class topic, gifted pupils could be encouraged to create their own book or leaflet for a specified audience on the topic at a more challenging depth. They can use information technology facilities and library sources for research purposes,

and can be taught good skimming and scanning techniques in using more detailed texts. The end-product can be presented to the whole class or year group as an end-of-topic summary.

2    During science sessions, gifted pupils can be encouraged to link their ideas across subjects and develop learning to the next level. For example, in learning about circuits the gifted child may be encouraged to design and build an alarm system. This would use their knowledge of circuits but link it with design and technology.

3    During numeracy sessions, where children are being taught calculation methods, a gifted child can be encouraged to investigate how many ways he/she can reach the same answer, exploring previous work covered and also encouraging more complex thinking.

4    Self-assessment is increasingly being encouraged across all year groups for all children. However, gifted pupils can be taught self-assessment and analytical skills.

5    Allow plenty of opportunities for the gifted pupil to verbalise their methods and ideas, particularly in numeracy. It is one skill to be able to come up with a correct answer and know in your head how you did it, but it is another to be able to explain it to others. Ensure you value their higher-level working. You may choose to have a 'methods' board for aspects of numeracy or science you are studying as a class. By displaying all methods you are able to value the level of understanding of all, including the more gifted pupils.

6    Use open-ended questions that allow more imaginative thought rather than set answers. All children can be encouraged to keep a questions book where they jot down things they would like to know about a topic.

7    Allow some free research time. During such times they can be encouraged to use the Internet, library and discussions in order to find answers to their own questions. This encourages independent learning which is important in later life. Classrooms are all too often places of fixed learning where outcomes are determined by adults and by SATs tests.

8    For the benefit of all subjects a 'Premiership League' list of words and definitions can be kept on the classroom wall and added to over the year. These words are ones which are good-quality alternatives, for example, 'pleasant' rather than 'nice'. Gifted pupils with a good command of language can support the learning of others by supplying some of the good alternatives.

## Activity 10.3

Are there any gifted and/or talented pupils in your class? Find out. Discuss with your class teacher the specific needs of these particular pupils and how he or she supports them. Does the SENCO have a role in this support? Who else might be involved? Draw up a list of strategies used.

# English as an additional language (EAL)

Although having English as an additional language is a different need and requires specific responses it is not to be considered a difficulty. In the 2001 Code of Practice for Special Educational Needs it states:

> Children must not be regarded as having a learning difficulty solely because the language or form of language of their home is different from the language in which they will be taught. (p.12)

Having a child or children in your class with English as an Additional Language should be seen as a cultural and educational opportunity for all the children and not a problem for them to get over. Some children may appear to have good use of the English language but this can be deceptive as there is more to language than speaking. A child may appear to be able to use the language well but may not fully understand what is said to him/her. This is especially so when more technical terms are used as part of subjects such as science and geography. Socially, they may have difficulties understanding cultural differences and/or local accents and phrases. These children are often quiet members of the class, especially when new to a school, and their needs and difficulty with understanding can be overlooked when other children with more challenging behaviour are demanding attention. Quiet does not necessarily indicate understanding or lack of anxiety.

It is also important to confirm with the family which language is the child's dominant language and whether they are being taught any additional languages at home or in their place of worship. This was something I learned while teaching in Durham. A boy entered our Reception class and it was initially indicated that the child's language at home was Urdu. After a short while in school we were concerned that the child was having great difficulties understanding what was going on in class despite additional support. With the help of the EAL support team we discovered that the child did speak Urdu at home but was also learning an additional two languages at his place of worship in order to read religious texts, and of course was trying to learn English at school. The child was four years old and trying to learn four languages simultaneously. It was no wonder he was finding things very difficult in school.

Although the Code of Practice makes it clear that English as an additional language is not a learning difficulty in itself, it also makes it clear that children with EAL may also have specific learning difficulties in addition, and these will be more difficult to identify early on.

# Standards for qualified teachers

To be recommended for and awarded Qualified Teacher Status (QTS) you must demonstrate that you can differentiate your teaching 'to meet the needs of pupils, including those with SEN'. This requirement is taken from the Standards for Qualified

Teacher Status (DfES 2002) and the Induction Standards for Qualified Teachers (DfES 2003). The Standards also require that you 'understand your responsibilities under the SEN Code of Practice and know how to seek advice from specialists on less common types of SEN'. In addition, you should be able to 'identify and support pupils who experience behavioural, emotional and social difficulties'. Intimidating as this may seem, you are not alone in these tasks and it is also the responsibility of the school's Special Educational Needs Co-ordinator (SENCO), head teacher and governing body to provide you with appropriate training, information and support in order for you to fulfil these requirements. It is unreasonable to expect you to be an expert on all different needs the moment you receive your degree and qualified teacher status. Some of this knowledge will come from your own experiences but much can be learned from the experiences of colleagues and specialists.

## Learning styles and different needs

We all have a preferred learning style even if we are not aware of it. What is more, it is likely that the children in your class will also have learning styles, although these may still be in the developmental stages.

> Educationalists and Psychologists now agree that children with specific learning difficulties exhibit a number of differences in their learning style to the majority of their classroom peers . . . they therefore require this work to be presented in a manner better suited to their learning style. (Wheeler 1997: 20)

There are three main styles: Visual, Auditory and Kinaesthetic. There may be some overlap in these styles in that someone may be a visual/kinaesthetic learner, for example. Smith (1996), in his series of books on accelerated learning, suggests that 29 per cent of the population are visual learners, 34 per cent are auditory and 37 per cent kinaesthetic. He would suggest that we do the majority of our learning and experience the world through our preferred learning style or dominant modality:

> learner goals are most effective when first described in the dominant modality or modalities. We all experience the world around us through our senses . . . through our preferred system of learning we interpret and re-interpret our everyday experiences. (p.34)

- Visual learners learn best through information presented visually, that is, with the use of diagrams, colours and shapes.

- Auditory learners flourish when information is presented via speech and sound.

- Kinaesthetic learners respond better through movement and the use of their senses.

Classrooms have, traditionally, been predominantly auditory and visual environments. Children do a lot of listening and looking but tend not to be too active in their learning unless a subject lends itself to practical activities, as with science and design & technology.

Many children with learning difficulties find auditory learning very difficult. In fact, there is a high incidence of children on special needs registers appearing to respond better to visual and kinaesthetic activities rather than auditory ones. In some previous research I undertook in Liverpool, using learning style questionnaires and interviews, I investigated the preferred learning styles of a group of 14 children with varied, but specific, learning difficulties. Of the 14, four were predominantly kinaesthetic learners, seven were visual/kinaesthetic learners and three were visual. None were auditory learners (Hume 2001). This kind of statistic needs to be borne in mind when considering your teaching style. Teaching needs to contain elements of all three learning styles in order that no child is denied access to the information being presented. This idea is echoed in the SEN Code of Practice where it states that all primary schools should consider the range of options and the variety of activities available within the class setting to enable children to access the National Curriculum. Teachers' planning should be flexible in order to recognise the needs of all children as individuals and to ensure progression, relevance and differentiation (DfES 2001: 53).

## Different responses

> We need to provide a personalised education that brings out the very best in every child, that builds on their strengths, enables them to develop a love of learning, and helps them to grow into confident and independent citizens, valued for the contribution they make. (DfES 2004)

It would be an impossible task to respond to the needs of every pupil at all times but there are many strategies and resources which can help all children access what you are trying to teach, instructions and the complexities of classroom life. Below you will find a small range of ideas and practical suggestions that may help you through teaching practice and your probationary period.

Earlier I mentioned the importance of learning styles and this is the key to good classroom organisation and teaching. Having activities and elements of each learning style within the context of each lesson will ensure that every child can access at least part of every lesson. Learning styles are also crucial in ensuring all children can understand and follow your instructions and the routines of the classroom.

Many children do not just have difficulties with learning but also in negotiating the sometimes confusing school and classroom environment. Teachers can often become quite exasperated by the child who cannot follow a simple instruction, and the child who does not have the materials they need for the lesson ready on time. Many of these children find it difficult to take in verbal information and to block out everything else which is going on in the classroom in order to focus on what is being said. Visual aids may seem very infantile but have proved to be very successful in supporting children with special needs within the context of a mainstream classroom.

## Case study 10.1: Tracey

In my role as SEN co-ordinator in a school in Durham I became very aware that the same children were having difficulty following instructions in every classroom every day, and these children, on the whole, were the same ones who had specific learning difficulties and required much of their work presented visually. We decided to experiment with a series of visual cue cards for key instructions. Every class teacher was given a pack of A4 cards with one picture and word/phrase on each. For example, one had a picture of an ear on it with the word 'listen' written underneath. The children were taught that for as long as the teacher was holding up the card they were meant to be listening. The teacher also said the instruction so that two learning styles were being used simultaneously. The cards became a visual focus and we discovered that many other children benefited from their use. There was now no excuse for not understanding or hearing an instruction, it also made expectations clear. Similar cards were created for 'look', 'put your pencil down', 'sit down' and similar instructions. The cards are a useful but simple way of supporting EAL children too, as they reduce the amount of understanding of English that is needed and also introduce them to the single instruction words in print.

Smaller cards were also produced for task instruction strips. Many children with learning difficulties have difficulty following more than one instruction at a time but activities are often made up of at least three or four instructions. We produced long strips of cards with Velcro™ on and cards with common task instructions on. For example, for a task that required children to colour a picture, cut it out and stick it in their book, a task board would be produced with a picture of a crayon colouring in, another with scissors, then a final one with a glue stick. The added advantage for all pupils is that this helps the children to become more independent in the classroom. Teachers can get worn down by the familiar cry 'What do I do next, Miss?' 30 times in the space of five minutes, as every child seems to forget the instructions you gave out at the beginning of the lesson three times, when they all assured you they had heard and understood. These kinds of visual supports are not going to harm the learning of any child. Good auditory learners will just not take much notice of them; but for the children who find listening very difficult it enables them to succeed and become more independent, relying less on an adult and providing them with opportunities for success. Again, this method of sequencing tasks will support EAL children in their understanding of what is expected of them.

Worksheets can also be supplemented with small visual images. Sometimes we present children with an A4 double-sided worksheet with many different sorts of activities involved in completing it – for example, reading, thinking, writing, listening, stop and wait. Small visual images can be inserted where instructions are written. This kind of support will not only help the visual learners but also support those children who have difficulty reading. It will also help children with dyslexia who have difficulty isolating where on the sheet they are up to and with focusing on the specific tasks, as their eyes and brain have problems keeping place and filtering out that which is irrelevant.

In order to help children in the Durham school who had difficulty with organising their own materials for each lesson and knowing what comes next, and those with autistic spectrum disorders who need to know what and when events are happening in order to reduce anxiety, we introduced a visual timetable in every classroom. These were made by myself and a few parents and involved pictures to represent each subject/activity which occurred weekly on the timetable, with a word underneath. They were stuck onto an A3 laminated card with Velcro™ and placed in a prominent part of the classroom. Each morning the class teacher would verbalise what was on the timetable to draw everyone's attention to it. Initially, we put them up for the children with ASDs but we soon found that many of the children were finding them helpful; so much so that there were times when children would point out to the teacher when they were not doing what was on it! It was especially helpful to our children who found organisation difficult. They could self-check what was coming next rather than having to remember or ask and get out the things they needed, e.g. PE kit. We also found that our ASD children were regularly checking the timetable and seemed more content with what was happening. There were obviously times when there were going to be uncertain events. When this was the case we stuck a red question-mark on the timetable and this appeared to be sufficient to reduce anxiety.

## Other things to try

A simple but effective support is photocopying your worksheets onto various pastel-coloured paper. Reading black print on white paper is actually the most difficult combination despite being the most common form of print. Children with specific learning difficulties such as dyslexia, dyspraxia and ASD can have difficulties with scotopic sensitivity, i.e. difficulty reading the black on white; the page can seem to glare, it can be quite painful on the eyes and can induce sickness and headaches. In more severe cases the print will appear to dance around the page or move round in circles making it almost impossible to read it effectively. It has been reported that the reading age of some children has improved by two years almost overnight when presented with text on coloured paper. By photocopying on pastel-coloured paper you remove a potential barrier for a few without hindering the rest. A similar support can be used on computers. By accessing the disability icon on your desktop you can alter the presentation of print from black on white to white on black, which can be of some help to these children.

Mind Maps™, developed by Tony Buzan, are an increasingly popular method of assessing and recording information for children. They can be used with children of all ages but are most successful in the primary phase with Year 2 children upwards. Put simply, Mind Maps are a visual way of recording information in a way that is personal to each mind mapper. Mind Maps are made up of words, pictures, lines and symbols that connect ideas and provide visual prompts for memory. For non-visual learners they can reduce the amount of visual images required but will still be a fun way of presenting thoughts or information. For visual/kinaesthetic learners they are an amazing aid to memory and way of recording thoughts and ideas.

Mind Maps are also a useful method of assessment. I have used mind mapping a great deal as a means of assessing how much some of the children with more complex needs knew before a topic and afterwards. Assessment is an important tool in monitoring the progress of SEN and EAL children and for setting realistic targets. For example, I started a Mind Map on the topic on Plants with a Year 2 child with autism. The child was encouraged to tell me anything and everything that he knew about plants. Within this I had a few key questions which I would ask based on the learning outcomes for the class. The child's responses were recorded on the Mind Map as well as any drawings he wished to do to illustrate his understanding. At the end of the topic I did a similar exercise, asking the same questions and asking him to tell me everything he knew about plants. With these two Mind Maps I was able to compare pre- and post-knowledge and target new areas for learning.

Allowing sufficient time for activities is crucial for children with special needs or EAL. Insufficient time can lead to lowering of self-esteem and frustration which can, in turn, lead either to reluctance to undertake tasks or to behaviour problems. Children need to know what is expected of them within the time and can often find a visual representation of how much time they have useful. For example, you could try pointing out on the clock when they will be asked to stop, or provide some children with a sand or digital timer and explain exactly how much work you expect to be done in the set time. Many children with SEN have problems with the concept of the passing of time; saying they have five minutes may mean nothing to them and result in incomplete tasks.

If you are setting the same piece of work for the whole class but you are not expecting the same amount of completed work from every child, the children may find it helpful if you put a line or coloured mark where you expect them to get to on the page or worksheet. This sets reasonable expectations for a range of abilities without having to produce half a dozen different sheets.

Praise and encouragement are probably the two greatest factors in getting the most out of any child, or adult for that matter. Nobody responds to constant negativity, but everyone can respond to positive comments and encouragement. There should always be something that you can find in a child's work that you can praise. While working as an SEN teacher in Liverpool I developed a system of assessment and target setting with my children that helped identify areas of weakness but balanced them with positive comments. Every child had a copy of our group checklist for good work, for example, remembering full stops, checking work, good vocabulary, underlined titles, etc. After every piece of written work I would sit down with each child individually for a few minutes and help them to evaluate their own work from the checklist. We would write on the facing page all the positive elements. Sometimes this was as simple as 'I have remembered the initial letters of most of the words'. Underneath we would write two targets for the next piece which would build on current success. This resulted in the children's good understanding of what is considered good writing and allowed them to feel positive about what they had produced and happy to work on the next step forward. Work consistently improved and basics were forgotten less often. This again helps develop independent learning even for children who have quite complex difficulties.

Where possible, it is always advisable to try to start from a child's area of interest. This is particularly true for children who find motivation and concentration difficult.

Allow them to work on a particular lesson focus but use a motivating theme. For example, I taught a bright child in Liverpool who had dyslexia, which hindered him a great deal and had lowered his confidence and concentration. He had fallen behind his peers and was being withdrawn in a small group for Literacy and Numeracy. At the beginning of the year I asked every child what they wanted to be when they grew up. This boy said he wanted to work with sharks, crocodiles and snakes, just like a famous Australian presenter. I found some books in the library and in shops on his beloved creatures. When we did work on poetry I would ask him to write something based on an image from one of the books. In writing stories I asked him to use a picture as a setting. In non-fiction he would, of course, write about snakes and sharks, which he enjoyed. His confidence and motivation improved 100 per cent and he produced some excellent work. By the end of the school year he was back working with his peer class in Literacy. A little motivation goes a long way.

Finally, allowing as many opportunities for the children to get up and move around (with purpose, of course), use their senses and bodies to enhance their learning, will go a long way to motivate and ensure understanding in your pupils. Kinaesthesia is vital in many areas of learning for all children. You will not easily teach someone to tie his/her shoe laces with just a series of verbal instructions. You would show them the laces, demonstrate, allow them to have a go, allow mistakes and give encouragement. The person has to physically try it in order to learn how to do it. The same goes for many learning goals in school, and all too often we rely too heavily on verbal instructions and demonstration and miss the 'try-it-yourself' stage. Movement in the classroom has to be controlled, and will be if your instructions are clear, activities are fun and expectations are clear. One colleague successfully taught times tables to Key Stage 2 children by touching various parts of the body as they recited each table. Having numbered tiles on the floor where children work through a times table can help a child keep his/her place (losing the place is a common difficulty with SEN children). They stand on number 1 and say 'one times five is five'. They then move onto number two and say 'two times five is ten', and so on. At the end of the number tiles I placed a poster of a fireworks display to signify achievement. It was a simple but effective way of maintaining interest in tables, which are not the most exciting elements of numeracy. Even moving around the room to work with a partner on the other side of the room can help. In today's fast-moving culture, children are used to being on the move and having things presented in short, bite-sized chunks. This is particularly so in children with many specific learning difficulties; sitting still for long periods is just not normal. Just think how you may have felt in some long, tedious lectures.

There has not been room in this chapter to provide you with a long list of activities and resources that can be used in individual subjects and activities. What I hoped to provide was a range of general strategies and resources that will support your pupils with special needs and EAL but not hinder the rest of the class. In fact, many may have a positive effect on them too. You will develop your own strategies and resources in time, with experience, but considering learning styles and some specific difficulties will make your early classroom life easier and will help you to see the potential for different approaches to teaching when planning your work.

## Conclusion

> We need to provide a personalised education that brings out the very best in every child, that builds on their strengths, enables them to develop a love of learning; and helps them to grow into confident and independent citizens, valued for the contribution they make. (DfES 2004)

There are no hard-and-fast answers to responding to different needs. There are basic principles, and you need to be prepared to be flexible and to constantly assess your own teaching against the progress of your pupils. Awareness that we are all individuals with different learning styles and individual combinations of strengths and weaknesses will take you half way to meeting those needs. You cannot make Oxbridge candidates out of all pupils, but what you *can* do is help each child to achieve their potential, whatever that is. In meeting the needs of one pupil and introducing new activities/resources for them you will support the needs of others. Throughout this chapter I have tried to provide activities, classroom strategies and further reading that aim to support as many pupils as possible in one go and which make your teaching less stressful. At the end of this chapter you will find a list of useful further reading (all of which is very practical rather than theoretical) and websites which provide activities and advice.

Finally, teaching children with different needs is an everyday reality of teaching. It is difficult and frustrating at times but it also makes your teaching career challenging, rewarding and varied.

## Suggestions for further reading

If you would like to explore some of the issues touched upon in this chapter, the following books should be of interest to you:

Buzan, T. (2003) *Mind Maps for Kids*. London: Thorsons.

Smith, A. (1996) *Accelerated Learning in the Classroom*. Stafford: Network Educational Press.

Smith, A. and Call, N. (1999) *The Alps Approach*. Stafford: Network Educational Press.

These books will provide you with more information on how to mind map and how to use the three main learning styles outlined in this chapter to motivate all the children in your class, not just the ones with special educational needs.

Westwood, P. (1997) *Commonsense Methods for Children with Special Needs* (3rd edn). London: Routledge.

This book provides you with a more general introduction to working with children with special educational needs in the mainstream classroom and contains ideas and strategies that may help in thinking about where and how to approach SEN.

## Useful websites

### SEN

www.geocities.com/sen_resources/resources.html

www.dfes.gov.uk

www.teachernet.gov.uk/wholeschool/sen

### Gifted and talented

www.standards.dfes.gov.uk/giftedandtalented/

www.nc.uk.net/gt/index.html [QCA guidance]

## References

Buzan, T. (2002) *How to Mind Map*. London: Thorsons.

Buzan, T. (2003) *Mind Maps for Kids*. London: Thorsons.

Hume, T. (2001), 'The effects of a kinaesthetic approach to teaching irregular spelling for a group of Year 3 and 4 children with Specific Learning Difficulties' (unpublished MA dissertation, Liverpool John Moores University).

Pollock, J. and Waller, E. (1994) *Day-to-Day Dyslexia in the Classroom*. London: RoutledgeFalmer.

Smith, A. and Call, N. (2001) *The Alps Approach Resource Book*. Stafford: Network Educational Press.

Wheeler, M. (1997) 'How have multi-sensory teaching programmes developed and why?' (unpublished MA dissertation, Liverpool John Moores University).

## Government documents and reports

Department for Education and Employment (DfEE) (1996) *Education Act – Chapter 56, Part IV, chapters 1 and 2*. London: HMSO.

Department for Education and Skills (DfES) (2001) *The Code of Practice for Special Educational Needs*. London: HMSO.

Department for Education and Skills (DfES) (2004) *Removing Barriers to Achievement – The Government's Strategy for SEN*. London: HMSO.

www.dfes.gov.uk/rsgateway [once into this site, look under the heading Special Education Needs, Special Needs Education] (Government Education Statistics DfES 2003).

www.dyspraxiafoundation.org.uk

www.nimh.nih.gov [National Institute of Mental Health]

www.dfes.gov.uk

www.nc.uk.net/gt/general/05_environment.htm [QCA guidance on Gifted and Talented Pupils]

www.tta.gov.uk [Teacher Training Agency]

www.teachernet.gov.uk/teachingginengland/ [Advice on teaching Gifted and Talented pupils]

# 11

# Personal, Social and Health Education and Citizenship

## Linda Johnston

## Introduction

Imagine a primary school where the focus is on developing academic excellence. At Key Stage 1 the children are drilled in phonics and aspects of numeracy while staff insist that all must write simple, punctuated sentences before the end of the Reception year. Whole-class teaching is the norm throughout the school with no time or opportunity for group or paired work. Experimentation, investigation and exploration are discouraged as they are time-consuming and a more efficient didactic approach is preferred. Thankfully, this rather Dickensian version of primary schooling is relegated to the history books in most establishments. True, the pressure of end-of-key-stage assessment has meant that 'teaching to the tests' has become a moral dilemma, but most teachers firmly believe that there is more to education than literacy and numeracy and to deprive children of a varied, balanced curriculum is doing them a disservice. Against such a backdrop, Personal, Social and Health Education and Citizenship (PSHE&C) provides children with life-enriching, developmental opportunities and experiences that may not be found elsewhere in the curriculum.

## What is Personal, Social and Health Education and Citizenship?

So what is PSHE&C? Buck and Inman (1991) state that

> Personal and social development involves engaging pupils in thinking about, inquiring into, discussing and confronting issues that have, simultaneously, profound importance both at a deep personal level and at a societal and global level.

Debates and discussions can take place in other parts of the curriculum, but the topics for discussion may be very different in PSHE&C. Children can be given the opportunity to discuss and explore problems that they themselves are experiencing as opposed to issues related to a geography or history topic. A number of approaches can be used to engage pupils in such debate.

# Circle time

In many primary schools circle time is the forum that is used to discuss issues that affect children's lives, such as bullying, jealousy or anxiety over tests. Jenny Mosley (1993) says that circle time is 'a democratic and creative approach used to consider a wide range of issues affecting the whole community, teaching staff, children, support staff, parents and governors'. During circle time everyone sits in a circle to promote good eye contact and to ensure that there is no hierarchy in the positioning of class mates. Often, games begin a session to ensure that everyone is involved and relaxed. An object (a shell, a stone) is passed around the circle and only when holding the object is a child permitted to speak. Rounds of this kind usually begin with simple sentences such as 'my favourite colour is . . .'. Once everyone has had a turn it is then possible to mix the children up by asking all children who said that 'blue' was their favourite colour to swap seats.

Circle times need a set of clearly defined rules that should be agreed with the class beforehand. They should include statements that protect the children and encourage a caring environment. For example, 'we never laugh at each other' and 'we think carefully before we talk about something personal' are useful rules. The rules should be discussed with the class before each session to reinforce their importance.

One means of addressing problems which children may be experiencing is through circle time:

> given opportunities appropriate to their age, intellectual and emotional development, children are clearly competent at expressing coherent views on a very wide range of important social, economic and personal issues, including issues of a deeply sensitive kind or where the children themselves may be disadvantaged by their own social, physical, intellectual or emotional circumstances. (Craig, in Hallet and Prout 2003)

Problem-solving activities addressed in circle times might be, 'How will we make sure that everyone has a fair turn in caring for the hamster?' in KS1, or 'Agony Aunt' responses to letters, real or fictional, in KS2. Children enjoy discussing solutions to moral dilemmas.

## Activity 11.1

When in school, arrange with your class teacher to carry out a discussion with a selected group of KS2 pupils. For example, they could be given the following scenario. Make sure they realise it is an invented one.

> The head teacher is cross because someone has marked his/her new car. You were near the car park and saw your favourite teacher accidentally reverse into it and then hurry away. What do you do?

How do the children respond? Reflect on this in the light of the earlier comments.

By collectively examining such issues, children can learn that they have choices and that actions result in some sort of reaction. Hopson and Scally (1981) conclude that 'None of the alternatives in some situations may be desirable, but it is the knowledge that there is always a choice that heralds the beginning of self-empowered thinking'.

## Developing a PSHE&C curriculum

Clearly, children need to have self-confidence in order to make choices. This can be developed through PSHE&C. A well-balanced PSHE&C curriculum provides opportunities for children to get to know themselves and their peers better. Their qualities can be publicly celebrated and help can be provided for perceived areas of weakness. Dowling (2000) states,

> One of the most important gifts we can offer young children is a positive view of themselves. Without this they will flounder throughout life and can be constantly seeking reassurance from others as they cannot seek it from within.

Self-esteem is a vital component for the general wellbeing of a person and it impacts on the ability of a child to learn. Is a child with low self-esteem likely to answer questions, ask for help, volunteer to take a lead role in a project or seek challenge in their school life? Probably not, and a wide range of learning opportunities are then lost.

### Activity 11.2

Observe the children in your class for several different lessons throughout the school day. Note how they interact – ask and answer questions, seek help, volunteer to do things, and so on. Do different children behave any differently in different lessons (i.e. different subjects)? What does this tell you about their self-esteem?

PSHE&C should include regular occasions for children to work together in small groups and pairs, thus enabling the less-confident children to participate. They can explore topics such as 'people who are kind to us in class' and 'things that I am good at'. This often works best if children are given plenty of time to think beforehand. Another way to promote self-esteem is to ask each child to write on separate pieces of paper what they feel each class member is good at. They can include 'You are very funny and are good at making me laugh' and 'You let me play football – you're good at sharing'. This is done anonymously and then all papers are distributed. Children are allowed to read the comments once everyone has sat down again. It is lovely for children to receive positive feedback about themselves and, as the comments are on paper, they can be kept and referred to later.

Dowling goes on to say that 'It is now very clear that unless a child achieves at least a minimal level of social competence by about the age of six, he or she is at risk for the rest of his or her life'. Careful planning can ensure that activities in PSHE&C can help to develop social skills in young children. As the range and nature of social interactions become more complex as we get older; then, clearly, the need for continuing the work begun at Foundation stage throughout primary schooling (and indeed beyond) is obvious.

## The citizenship dimension

PSHE&C is not simply about developing a clearer understanding of the self; it is also concerned with what each individual can contribute to society as a whole. It is about ensuring that children understand that everyone has rights that we should respect and uphold. This is the 'citizenship' part of PSHE&C.

In the QCA guidance (2000) it states that the Citizenship Framework

emphasises the development of social and moral responsibility, community involvement and some of the basic aspects of political literacy, for example, knowing what democracy is and about the basic institutions that support it locally and nationally, as essential preconditions of citizenship as well as PSHCE.

## The place of the class or school council

But how do schools put this into practice? One way forward is the development of class and school councils which are now becoming more commonplace in primary schools. The *Primary School Councils Toolkit* (Clay and Gold 2002) gives invaluable tips on how to establish a council and provides photocopiable training materials for both staff and children.

A school council gives children an insight into democratic proceedings as members are usually elected by secret ballot. Some schools even require children to campaign beforehand to make sure that they gain the support of their peers. As meetings are usually of a formal nature they have a proper agenda and minutes and are led by an elected chairman. Ideally, the council should have a budget so that children learn financial management at first hand. Elected representatives from each class or year group are given the responsibility of relaying information from the meeting back to the class. It is usual for a member of the senior management team to attend the meetings (and often act as secretary), but in some cases governors and other staff are invited.

### Activity 11.3

Does the school you are in operate a school council? If so, ask permission from the head teacher to attend to see how it operates and how the pupils take responsibility within it.

Issues discussed at school councils range from improving the playground facilities to organising a disco. Often funds are raised through sponsored events but this should not be an overriding function of a school council. Its status should be recognised by reporting action to parents in newsletters and to governors in the head teacher's report.

Research by Taylor and Johnson (2002) determined that through involvement in a school council children develop 'a greater sense of ownership and increased understanding of management issues, as well as enhancing problem-solving activities and improving behaviour'. Buck *et al.* (2003) also felt that 'School councils can contribute to a more inclusive school and form part of a range of strategies to combat disaffection and alienation of some pupils'. This is partly because school councils have no academic bias and are not reliant on the contributions of any one person. Indeed, there is a corporate responsibility for the successful working of a school council that lies with the whole school. School and class councils, then, provide an important vehicle for promoting personal development; they are a means of delivering part of the Citizenship curriculum and they can and should lead to school improvement.

It should be noted that school councils and circle time form only part of what PSHE&C is all about, but they are a valuable part.

## Why develop a PSHE&C curriculum?

The previous section outlined what PSHE&C is and indicated some of the educational benefits that can be gained by following a carefully planned curriculum. There is no statutory requirement, however, to teach PSHE&C, but there is an expectation that aspects are addressed. In the National Curriculum (DfEE 2000) document this expectation is made quite clear:

> The school curriculum should promote pupils' spiritual, moral, social and cultural development and, in particular, develop principles for distinguishing between right and wrong . . . The school curriculum should pass on enduring values, develop pupils' integrity and autonomy and help them to be responsible and caring citizens capable of contributing to the development of a just society.

This clearly acknowledges that aspects of personal and social development cannot be left to chance but should be part of a structured programme of learning. However, finding time to deliver PSHE&C can be difficult as the timetables of most primary schools are full to overflowing. Mercifully, the DfES document *Excellence and Enjoyment* (2003) gives permission and illustrates ways in which schools can address the curriculum more creatively, thus making time for PSHE&C. Buck *et al.* (2003) identify the following ways of planning PSHE&C:

- teaching PSHE within the National Curriculum subjects;
- PSHE as a topic;

- PSHE as a strand within a topic;
- a timetabled PSHE slot;
- PSHE as an 'experiential' challenge;
- circle time.

They then go on to discuss the advantages and disadvantages of each. No single planning strategy, however, would meet all the needs of a well-balanced PSHE&C curriculum. Regular circle-time sessions of between 30 and 45 minutes should be timetabled so that children develop the feeling that it is important and that their views matter. It also means that issues can be addressed promptly and the skills of 'good listening' are regularly rehearsed.

## PSHE&C across the curriculum

When preparing medium-term plans, teachers usually aim to form as many cross-curricular links as is reasonably possible. There are many opportunities for addressing aspects of PSHE&C through other areas of the curriculum. Examining the media for evidence of bias and discrimination in Literacy; debating the proposed development of a retail park in Geography; and reflecting on the cultural changes brought about in Britain following the invasion and settlement of the Vikings in History are means of addressing aspects of PSHE&C, within a specific context.

Topics and theme weeks, such as 'Ourselves' or 'Keeping Healthy', provide ideal opportunities to focus on areas of PSHE&C, such as 'Relationships and Sex Education', which can otherwise be difficult to plan in. Visitors can be booked in advance to assist with the delivery of the topic (nurse, dentist, nutritionist) and resources can be gathered/ordered for a particular block of time.

Ideally, a weekly or fortnightly slot for PSHE&C can be planned in. This enables particular skills to be practised frequently and allows the teacher to monitor progress on a more regular basis. There are commercial schemes that can provide ideas to explore within these sessions, but they should be used very selectively. It is generally better to devise a scheme of work that is relevant to your particular school, with the needs of your children in mind.

## Transforming theory into practice

For PSHE&C to have a positive and lasting impact on children's lives it is essential that lessons take place within a caring, supportive environment. Hay McBer (2000) researched extensively into the effect that classroom climate has on children's ability to learn. In considering the impact that this climate has on the success of PSHE&C it was found that the element that was central to effective practice was the quality of the relationships between the participants. It is vital that children within a class are respected and are treated equally by you, the teacher. They cannot be expected to show courtesy to others unless they have a good role model to follow. McBer also concluded that PSHE&C 'can only take place in a relationship of trust and mutual respect, and in a learning environment that enables young people to feel good about themselves'.

Clearly, an environment that encourages the development of self-esteem is an essential ingredient for success. In developing this nurturing environment teachers must devise, preferably with the class, a set of behavioural rules and classroom routines. These need to be in line with a whole-school behaviour policy but should be explored with the children in the context of the classroom within which they are working. Rules that are explicit, are fully explained and are enforced consistently help to give children a feeling of security as boundaries and consequences become clear.

## Some golden rules

Jenny Mosley (1998) devised a set of 'Golden Rules' which are used widely throughout primary schools. These are written as positive instructions, such as, 'Do be kind and helpful'; 'Don't hurt people's feelings'. By including the behaviour to be avoided, the expectations regarding what children should and should not do are more explicit. These Golden Rules reflect the values held by the school and should not include operational directives such as 'Always walk in the corridor', which may be displayed separately.

For rules to be enforced effectively, sanctions and rewards should be in place. Jenny Mosley (1998) advocates the use of 'Golden Time' as a means of rewarding those who have kept the Golden Rules. This is a strategy that I have used and which I have found to be effective. All children begin the week with a full half-hour of Golden Time (or more/less depending on agreed procedures). They choose activities that they would like to do, such as playing with the parachute, playing board games, watching a video or playing on scooters brought from home. Lessons then proceed as normal. Children who are following the rules should be praised frequently (a wink, thumbs up, a discreet pat on the back), while those who break a rule lose Golden Time. Initially, they lose five minutes, but further infringements result in more time being deducted in five-minute blocks. Sometimes children don't really understand what it is that they have done to break a rule and so it is always important to clarify this with the child. They then have the right to earn it back by entering into a contract with the teacher. Juniors can often suggest ways of making amends but children in Key Stage 1 may need more guidance.

This system, or modifications of it, works for most children and is popular in schools because it takes a very positive view of children's behaviour and contributes to creating a positive ethos. As they begin the week with all of the Golden Time intact, there is the shared assumption that they can behave and can keep the rules. If they do break a rule they can still redeem themselves. This reduces the likelihood of children being labelled as 'naughty', which causes real damage to self-esteem. Those who constantly lose Golden Time need individual help and may well be following targets from their Individual Education Plan.

Following on from the Golden Rules and Golden Time system I developed a 'Golden Book' for my class. This is a large scrapbook covered in gold holographic paper and stands on a special, covered table. All of the children's achievements, awards and certificates are noted in this book. There are certificates that have been awarded by the Playground Guardians, playtime awards and some certificates that children have received for out-of-school activities. I devised additional certificates to encourage the children to take pride in their classroom and in themselves. Each day the cleaner signs a small 'Tidy Class' award if no pencils, rubbers etc. have been left on the floor, and supply staff have a special certificate to sign if the children have worked and behaved well. By the end of the school year the class Golden Book is full of positive feedback for each child (careful recording can ensure that this happens). When days are not going well, or a child is struggling to follow the rules, it is useful to share the book with the children as a reminder of all of the good things that they have achieved and can achieve.

Encouraging children to reflect on their own success is important. They need to recognise for themselves when they have worked or behaved well, otherwise they will constantly seek reassurance. With this in mind I developed a 'Good Work' wall in class. Each week six children select a piece of work for display of which they are proud (work in books can be photocopied). They explain why they have chosen the work and it is then displayed for a week. A simple tick list on a class record sheet ensures that everyone regularly has their turn. Although this is simple, and very easy to administer, it means that all children are encouraged to evaluate their own work and have it on display regularly.

## Some things to consider

When creating a classroom climate that is conducive to the success of PSHE&C it is important to consider a number of points:

- Create a class rota so that everyone has the opportunity to do jobs.

- How will children know where resources are kept? Computer-printed labels with a picture are very helpful but children still need to be taught where everything is.

- How will you establish routines? Some, such as lining up for assemblies, are worth practising with children so they know exactly what is expected of them.

- Does your style of teaching accommodate all kinds of learners?

- How will you begin and end the day with the class so that they develop the feeling that you care about their wellbeing? One way is to ask each child how they are feeling at the beginning of the day. My class does this during registration and they have assigned a colour to each feeling. This has provided me with invaluable information about my children. Sometimes they are grey (sad) because dad has to work away from home for a while or they may be lilac (excited) because their team is playing a match that day. With this knowledge children can be dealt with more sensitively and sympathetically. End the day with joke-telling, a favourite class story or reflect on the best parts of the day.

There is so much to take into account when setting up classroom procedures. If these are established at the very beginning of the school year, however, and are taught and rehearsed with the children, it helps to create a climate in which PSHE&C can thrive.

## Games and activities for use in PSHE&C

Initially, children need to learn that PSHE&C is fun, relevant to them and timetabled to take place each week. Games, ice-breakers and 'getting-to-know-you' activities can be used at the beginning of the school year when the class is still new to you. Examples of such activities include:

- *This Is Your Life*. Children work in random pairs and opt to be A or B. A tells B three facts about themselves (or more/less depending on the age and ability of the children) and vice versa. When reporting back to the class children have to recall the facts that they have heard.

- *All About Me*. Children complete booklets about their likes/dislikes, hobbies and dreams for the future.

- *Find someone who . . . .* Children are given the task of finding someone who, for example, has a pet rabbit, a yellow bedroom or a sister. This develops communication skills and allows children to learn about classmates with whom they do not interact on a regular basis.

Similar activities can be used at any time during the year and are good ice-breakers at the beginning of a session. Activities that I have found to be popular are:

- *Hunt the Hippo*. A child leaves the room or covers her eyes while another hides the hippo (or any other small cuddly toy). This game is played like 'colder and warmer' but as the 'hunter' nears the hippo the children clap loudly and quickly and if the child moves further away from the hippo the children clap more slowly and softly. The end result is that when the 'hunter' finds the hippo all of his/her classmates are clapping. This can be a great self-esteem booster as some children never hear their peers applauding them.

- *Ball Catch*. Children sit on chairs in a circle. A child stands in the middle and throws a foam ball in the air while saying the name of someone in the class (not a friend). The classmate then rushes into the circle to collect the ball (they aren't really expected to catch the ball, but some do).

- *Wink Murder*. A 'detective' has to deduce which child has been chosen to be the murderer, who claims his/her victims by winking at them. The detective is allowed three guesses.

- *Follow Me*. One child has to spot which child has been chosen to change the action that everyone else is copying (nodding, scratching, waving etc.).

There are many excellent ideas for PSHE&C in Curry and Bromfield's (1994) book *Personal and Social Education for Primary Schools through Circle Time* but children can also suggest games of their own.

## Discussion

Following games and similar activities it is then usual to explore a theme or an issue with the class. There are various ways of tackling this, such as circle time, which was discussed earlier, and discussion. This may be with the whole class but it usually works best if children are in small groups. Those who are reticent are more likely to contribute if there is a smaller audience. There are many stimuli that can be used for discussion:

- Puppets and soft toys – children, especially younger ones, enjoy interacting with the toys to solve their problems.
- Posters and photographs – portraits are useful for learning to recognise emotions.
- Stories and poems – these can present characters for 'hot seating' (see below).
- Newspapers and magazines – topical issues, such as football hooliganism, can be discussed.

## Debates

Children prepare arguments for or against issues, the enforcement of a curfew for under-sixteen-year-olds or legislation against smoking in public places for example. These are then presented to the class, usually with elected spokespersons.

## Hot seating

Volunteers take the 'hot seat' and become a specified character, such as Draco Malfoy from the Harry Potter stories. Everyone else can then question the character about their actions and motives.

## Drawing, writing, painting

Sometimes children should work on their own, in pairs or in very small groups so that more confident children do not dominate. They can compose replies to 'Agony Aunt' letters, add thought or speech bubbles to pictures or paint pictures of what it feels like to be bullied.

## Drama

Many themes explored in PSHE&C lend themselves to dramatic representation, but there is a risk that the drama can take over. To prevent this from happening, stop the action occasionally to analyse the behaviours and possible motives of characters as well as exploring the choices that they have when facing decisions.

The methods that you choose to deliver PSHE&C will depend on the focus for a particular session, the space available to you, your confidence and experience and the nature of your class. In order to keep PSHE&C alive for children it is important to use a range of techniques.

In the following case study, a variation on circle time was used to explore a problem that we were experiencing in class.

## Case study 11.1: Linda

### The context

I taught David (name changed) when he was a member of a 34-strong, mixed-ability Y4 class. I had been 'warned' about the class by its previous teacher who described it as being 'difficult'. Fights and squabbles were not uncommon and I had been called upon to act as mediator on a number of occasions. I was also aware that the ability level within the class ranged from insecure level 2s to secure level 5s and that there were a number of children with specific learning difficulties, and two with autism. I was determined, however, that the class would not get the better of me and that I would bring about positive change.

The autumn term began with high expectations. I had attended an inspiring course run by Jenny Mosley and I was armed with strategies that I felt would help to create a positive classroom climate. By the October half-term I was beginning to see progress and was thoroughly enjoying teaching this interesting mix of individuals. Each of them was a real 'character' but, of course, we still had our difficulties. Some of the girls fell in and out of friendship with depressing regularity. One boy cheerfully admitted that he just couldn't control his temper and another struggled to tell the truth whenever there was a remote chance that he might get into trouble. Most of these issues were tackled successfully by employing our Assertive Discipline Policy and PSHE strategies. David, however, was a different matter.

David was a likeable boy with general learning difficulties and a complex home life. He was loved by both parents but he found the constant friction between them hard to cope with. Eventually, they separated and David clearly had torn loyalties. Up to this point David's behaviour had been manageable. He frequently pestered and teased children at playtimes but would respond to sanctions and rewards. Now, however, with his home life in such disarray his behaviour deteriorated. Frequent complaints were made by children and staff about how David was deliberately hurting others, both physically and mentally. Clearly something had to be done, and after attempting a number of approaches I decided to enlist the help of the class.

### Finding a solution

Some time before one of our weekly circle time sessions I asked to speak to David. We discussed the fact that he was always in trouble and he admitted that he was not very happy. I then suggested that we ask the class for ideas of ways in which the situation could be improved. David was quite keen to try this and so it was scheduled for the next session.

With some trepidation I took a seat within the circle. We began with some warm-up games and then did two rounds of passing an object (an unusual stone) and completing 'I like it when people . . .' and 'I don't like it when people . . .' sentences. Then, I moved on to the focus for the session. I began by saying that David needed some help. He had developed a habit of hurting and pestering people and he didn't know how to stop. Would the class like to try to help him? Most of the children were very enthusiastic but some bore David such a grudge or were so frightened of him that they didn't want to help at this stage.

So that we had a shared understanding of what the issue was, I then asked the class to describe some of the things that David had done to hurt or upset them. A forest of hands appeared and a number of children were asked to describe what had happened to them. I felt that it was important for David to hear about the behaviours that were upsetting others and which had ultimately made him friendless. When asked if he recognised the incidents David admitted that he did.

Next came the crucial and most worrying part of the process: would the children be able to think of ways to help David or would they simply want to punish him? I decided to put David in charge. The children were asked if they had any sensible ideas that they could offer. David would consider each of them and if he thought they seemed reasonable, then I would write them on a large piece of paper. Several hands were raised and David chose which children would speak first. Ideas ranged from barring David from playtimes to making him walk around with the teacher on duty. Once we had collected a number of ideas each one was considered in turn. Again, David took the lead here and he commented on why ideas might or might not work. Other children joined in and noted that some ideas were not 'fair'.

One idea, however, grabbed David's attention. It was suggested that he had two 'minders' at playtimes who would keep an eye on him. They would play with David, if that was what he wanted (by now, David had no real friends and spent most playtimes alone) or they would simply take note of how he was behaving. At the end of break time the 'minders' would report back to me. David liked this idea; it appealed to him that he would have two guaranteed playmates each day and that I would get to hear about his progress. I was delighted that David had warmed to an idea but I was concerned about the reality of it working. Who would want to be his 'minders'?

With my heart in my mouth I asked if anyone would like to be David's minder. I was staggered by the response. Nearly all of the children, girls as well as boys, raised their hands. David looked really pleased, especially as some children were on the verge of exploding, desperate to be chosen. After some deliberation, David chose two boys.

As improvement of any kind needs to be measured, I asked the class how we could monitor David's progress. They suggested a 'smiley sheet' on which he would record with a tick each play session that had been positive. This would be done only once I had spoken with the minders. These ticks would then convert to points on our whole-school behaviour chart. The boys helping David would also earn points, as would anyone else who the minders noted were actively helping him.

The system was put into operation and was duly monitored. David didn't suddenly sprout wings and become angelic, but his behaviour improved enormously. At the end of one circle time session I asked the children who they would like to nominate for a special mention (something we occasionally do). Several children nominated David because he was 'much better now'. David, in turn, nominated the whole class, 'for helping me'.

## Reflections

This process was very successful in this instance but might well have foundered with a different group of children. There were, I feel, many valuable lessons to be learned:

for David:

- he can make choices;
- he doesn't have to solve problems on his own;
- people are prepared to forgive;

for the class:

- as members of a community they can bring about change;
- everyone deserves a chance;
- sharing a problem can lead to a solution;

for me, the teacher:

- I don't have to have all the answers;
- expect the best of everyone;
- children's enthusiasm can make things work.

I have used similar problem-solving approaches with other classes since then, always with a degree of success. If children are treated as responsible members of the school community they will usually behave as such.

## Suggestions for further reading

If you would like to explore some of the issues touched upon in this chapter, the following books should be of interest to you:

Clay, D. and Gold, J. (2000) *Primary School Councils Toolkit*. London: School Councils UK.

Curry, M. and Bromfield, C. (1994) *Personal and Social Education in Primary Schools Through Circle-Time*. London: NASEN.

There are many excellent ideas in these two books for you to use as a starting point for PSHE&C work with your class.

# References

Buck, M. and Inman, S. (1991) *Curriculum Guidance No. 1: Whole School Provision for Personal and Social Development*. London: Centre for Cross-curricular Initiatives, Goldsmiths College.

Buck, M., Inman, S. and Tandy, M. (eds) (2003) *Enhancing Personal, Social and Health Education: Challenging Practice, Changing Worlds*. London: RoutledgeFalmer.

Clay, D. and Gold, J. (2000) *Primary School Councils Toolkit*. London: School Councils UK.

Curry, M. and Bromfield, C. (1994) *Personal and Social Education in Primary Schools Through Circle-Time*. London: NASEN.

Department for Education and Employment (DfEE) (2000) *The National Curriculum*. London: DfEE/HMSO.

Department for Education and Skills (DfES) (2003) *Excellence and Enjoyment: A Strategy for Primary Schools*. Nottingham: DfES.

Dowling, M. (2000) *Young Children's Personal, Social and Emotional Development*. London: Sage.

Hallet, C. and Prout, A. (eds) (2003) *Hearing the Voices of Children: Social Policy for a New Century*. London: RoutledgeFalmer.

Hopson, B. and Scally, M. (1981) *Lifeskills Teaching*. Maidenhead: McGraw-Hill.

McBer, H. (2000) *Research into Teacher Effectiveness*. London: DfEE.

Mosley, J. (1993) *Turn Your School Round*. Cambridge: LDA.

Mosley, J. (1998) *More Quality Circle Time, Volume 2*. Cambridge: LDA.

QCA (2000) *Personal, Social and Health Education and Citizenship at Key Stages 1 and 2*. London: Qualifications and Curriculum Authority.

Taylor, M. and Johnson, R. (2002) *School Councils: Their Role in Citizenship and Personal and Social Education*. Slough: NFER.

# 12

# The way ahead

## Eve English

## Introduction

By the time you've reached this chapter you should be well on your way to meeting the QTS standards and becoming a qualified teacher. This, however, is just the beginning. In front of you is a career in which you never stop thinking and learning. Your induction year will build on your Initial Teacher Training and prepare you for Continuing Professional Development (CPD), and we will look at that in this chapter. But first of all, we look at the issue of that important first job.

Because you will have to apply for teaching posts around January for the following September, you cannot afford to postpone applying for jobs because you have so many other things to think about. You must put as much effort into job applications and interviews as you have done into assignments and teaching practice.

## Applying for your first job

First of all, where do you want to teach? Do you want to stay near home, be close to the university where you've made lots of friends, or are you prepared to move any-where? Once you've decided where you want to teach find out how the local education authorities (LEAs) in that area advertise their jobs. The *Times Educational Supplement* can be invaluable in this respect. As schools now control their own budgets (because of Local Management of Schools arrangements), many advertise vacancies directly; others make use of LEA pools. As soon as you have decided on which posts or LEAs you are going to apply for, or to, then you will need to start thinking about a curriculum vitae (CV) and a letter of application. You may also be asked to complete an application form.

Most schools and LEAs will ask you to write a letter of application. It is a good idea to include one even if you are not asked. Although you will be applying for a number of posts at the same time you must ensure that each letter is different and makes reference

## Activity 12.1

Prepare a CV. This should present *relevant* information in as succinct a way as possible. Include important biographical details, qualifications and educational institutions, listed with the most recent first, other relevant experience and teaching experience (school placements). Personal interests can also help give an employer an idea of what you are like as a person. You should also include the names of two referees. These would normally be a university tutor and head teacher of the school in which you have completed a school experience. (Remember that you must ask permission of your referees to include their names.)

to the individual school and the information the school has sent you. If the school needs a teacher proficient in Information and Communication Technology, the head teacher and governors will want to know about your strengths in that area as well as your other abilities and talents. Perhaps your flexibility may be the best characteristic to stress. It can be very tempting to be creative in describing your strengths when you apply for jobs. However, be careful that you do not, for example, exaggerate your musical or PE skills or you may find yourself in a post that requires you to use your Grade 2 piano qualification to play for school assemblies, or one in which your interest in football (illustrated by your season ticket for the local football team) is seen as proof that you can take the school team to the top of the junior league. Be realistic but confident at the same time. Describe your school experiences and say what you learned from them. Tell them why you enjoy teaching and why you would fit into their particular school. Find out about the school by looking carefully through the information sent, but also look up the school's most recent Ofsted report. This can give you official information but can never give you the full picture. Always try to visit the school if possible and gauge the ethos and atmosphere.

## Case study 12.1

### The selection process

One primary head teacher describes how she selects candidates for posts in her school:

*My first priority is to select a good classroom practitioner. I may need someone who can eventually be a co-ordinator in a particular curriculum area but, first and foremost, I need someone who works well in the classroom. What do I mean by this? Relating well to children is essential. My teachers treat children with respect and I would want anyone joining the staff to be the same. I can still remember the teachers who bawled and shouted at the children and I wouldn't like that to happen again. A candidate's references often help me to find out about how he/she acts in the classroom but, increasingly, I ask candidates to work with the children on a prepared activity. This gives me as much insight into how they relate to children as it does into their curricular knowledge. I need to know about their classroom management and that they use positive strategies, wherever possible, to encourage good behaviour. I want to know that they are creative and imaginative in their teaching and that learning objectives are not the 'be all and end all'. I usually take candidates around the school individually. I used to take them round as a group but found that the group dynamics often prevented me from getting to know them. The governors and I still carry out formal interviews and we ask questions that will hopefully elicit thoughtful responses. We want to find out as much as possible about them; making the right appointment is so very important. Personality is important to us and so is the ability to think about issues. We don't want a teacher who thinks that QTS is the end of the educational process; we want someone who will be committed to the school and who will work hard (even though, as a head, I'd like to think I encourage my staff to have lives beyond school).*

*Questions that we have asked of candidates include:*

- *Describe one of your most rewarding and successful lessons. Why was it successful?*

- *Describe one of your least successful lessons. What went wrong?*

- *Where would you like to be in five years? How will you get to that position?*

- *What methods of organising and managing classrooms have you experienced? What was most successful?*

- *What are your main strengths as a teacher? Give examples.*

- *In what areas of the curriculum would you need support?*

  *Which subjects would you be able to co-ordinate, with support, after your induction year?*

- *Are there any extra-curricular areas that you would be able to contribute to?*

- *What difference do you think the National Primary Strategy will or should make to the curriculum?*

The case study above is fairly typical of the selection process. Increasingly, head teachers are asking candidates to plan and teach lessons to groups of children. This can be daunting and needs careful preparation. Try the activity below:

## Activity 12.2

Plan, for interview, a 30-minute lesson to teach to a particular age group from a curricular area of your choice. It will be a whole-class lesson. Identify, in your planning, the learning objective(s), activities, resources and key questions. Remember that you will not know the children and will need to ensure that your lesson can involve children of different abilities, so allow the lesson needs to be imaginative. Do not take too many risks.

It is often a good idea to leave planning for follow-up activities to your lesson.

The head teacher in the case study listed some possible interview questions. Questions at interview are usually aimed at finding out as much as possible about you as a person, as a teacher and as a potential subject co-ordinator. You will also need to be well-informed about current educational issues and initiatives and will need to have thought about these and have opinions.

Do not be disheartened if you are not successful at first. You may be a good candidate but perhaps someone was just a little better on the day or had strengths in areas needed by the school. Always agree to feedback if it is offered.

## Activity 12.3

**Preparing a portfolio**

In order to give the school as much information as possible about you as a teacher it can be very useful to prepare a portfolio to take with you to interview. Start building up this portfolio. It could include:

a brief CV;

examples of lesson plans;

photocopies of good observation reports by your school mentors or university tutors;

photographs of displays you have created; and

photocopies of children's work, appropriately marked.

## The induction year and career entry and development profiles

As you finish your Initial Teacher Training and are looking forward to your first job you will need to think about your induction year and your Career Entry and Development Profile. Since May 1999 (DfEE 1999) all newly qualified teachers have been required to complete an induction period of three school terms if they are to work in maintained primary or secondary schools in England. This follows and builds upon the award of Qualified Teacher Status (QTS) which is awarded on the satisfactory completion of a programme of initial teacher training (ITT). NQTs who are awarded QTS but who do not satisfactorily complete the statutory induction period will not be eligible for employment as a teacher in a maintained school. Circular 5/99 (*ibid.*) sets out the arrangements for the induction period and the induction standards against which NQTs will be assessed. The head teacher will be responsible for the assessment process (against the national standards for the completion of induction) but if he or she is not your induction tutor then some aspects of the assessment might be delegated to that tutor. You should have a number of formal interviews throughout the year. At the final review meeting the head should tell you whether or not you will be recommended as meeting the standards for successfully completing the induction period. The head will make this recommendation to the appropriate body, usually the LEA, and this body will make the final decision.

This may all sound like just something else to worry about but you must remember that, as well as ensuring that you meet the standards, the arrangements for induction mean that all NQTs get the support they need. It was not unknown for NQTs to be given a class register, shown their classroom and left to get on with it. Now the requirements are such that you, as an NQT, will get the support you require. This support begins with your Career Entry and Development Profile (CEPD).

As you come to the end of your initial teacher training you will be asked to complete a CEDP (Transition Point 1) (TTA 2003). This asks you to reflect on your time in the classroom, your strengths, what you found particularly interesting and rewarding in your teaching, your areas for development, where you might need more support, and also asks you to think about your future in teaching. This, in fact, is the beginning of your continuing professional development.

## Activity 12.4

Begin to think about the following:

At this stage, which aspect(s) of teaching do you find most interesting and rewarding?
What do you consider to be your main strengths as a teacher?
In what areas would you welcome more support and advice?
How would you like to see your teaching career develop?

Transition Point 2 (TTA 2003) is the start of your induction year. Your school induction tutor will help you build on the strengths you have identified in your CEDP and support you in the areas in which you feel that is needed. However, you will also be given information about the school and your role. Transition Point 2 was not included in the original version of the CEDP but the TTA responded to the request that the particular needs of individual schools should help shape the NQT's targets. There will also be the opportunity to bring to the discussion any additional experience you have had between the Transition Points 1 and 2.

Your school induction tutor will, therefore, discuss with you 'your priorities for induction and how these relate to, build on, or differ from the priorities you identified at Transition Point 1' (ibid.: 18). As with Transition Point 1 you will be asked to consider particular questions but you can change the format of the CEDP and add to the CEDP any information you think appropriate. The questions you are asked to consider are:

1  At the moment, what do you consider to be the most important professional development priorities during your induction period?

2  How have your priorities changed since Transition Point 1?

**3** How would you prioritise your needs across your induction period?

**4** What preparation, support or development opportunities do you feel would help you move forward with these priorities?

(ibid.: 18)

Transition Point 3 is towards the end of your induction period when you will be asked to look back on the period and consider how much you have achieved. You will also be asked to think of your continuing professional development. The suggested questions at this point are:

**1** Thinking back over your induction period, what do you feel have been your most significant achievements as a newly qualified teacher?

**2** How have you built on the strengths you identified at the end of your initial teacher training? What evidence is there of your progress in these areas?

**3** When you look back over your induction action plans and your records of review meetings, which objectives do you feel have been achieved and why?

**4** Have any of the objectives, aspirations and goals that you outlined at Transition Points 1 and 2 not been addressed during your induction period? How could you take these forward into the next stage of your career?

**5** Thinking ahead to the class(es) you will teach and the responsibilities you will be taking on next year, what do you feel are the priorities for your professional development over the next two or three years?

**6** What options are you currently considering for professional and career progression?

(ibid.: 24)

From the beginning of your induction process it is expected that you have support from a designated tutor and that you have regular review meetings, observations of your lessons and constructive feedback on these, opportunities to observe colleagues in your own school or perhaps other schools and other targeted development activities.

## Case study 12.2

S. is nearing the end of her induction year in a primary school and is looking back at Transition Points 1 and 2. She described assessment and target setting as being areas in which she did not feel confident and would appreciate support. Her school induction tutor used this as one of the targets for her action plan and linked it with extending the learning of more able children as this was a school priority (identified in the school's development plan). Non-contact time was used to analyse data with the help of the mentor. One of the strengths identified by the newly qualified teacher (NQT) at both Transition Points 1 and 2 was her teaching of English. This was built upon over the induction year by giving the NQT the opportunity to work alongside the English co-ordinator with the aim of possibly sharing that role in the future. She was able to attend courses both within and outside the school to address her concerns and build upon her strengths. She observed other teachers in her own school and in other schools and found this very helpful.

S's lessons were observed by her tutor, subject co-ordinators and the head teacher. She did not find this particularly daunting as she had become used to it during her Initial Teacher Training. She had regular meetings with her induction tutor and there was constructive feedback and further targets set.

S. was obviously well supported by her induction tutor/mentor. Being a mentor is an extremely important role and demands experience of all areas of a school's organisation as well personal qualities that include being positive and supportive.

Observing other teachers was described by S. as being very helpful and you will know from your ITT that this is certainly the case. You will also know that to be valuable the observation must be clearly focused.

## Becoming a subject co-ordinator

At the end of your successful induction year you may be asked to become a subject co-ordinator. If you are lucky you may co-ordinate a subject area in which you have a real interest but you might just as easily be asked to step in where there is a vacancy. Remember you are qualified to teach all subjects of the National Curriculum. It will be useful, during your school placements in your ITT year, to discuss the role of co-ordinator with members of staff.

### Activity 12.5

During your time in school, talk to co-ordinators about their role. Ask about:

- their part in the planning of their curriculum subject;
- their part in the assessment process;
- the monitoring of the teaching of their subject;
- the ordering of resources;
- extra-curricular work associated with their subject; and
- the delivery of in-service training.

The following case studies describe the role of the co-ordinator of a foundation subject and that of the co-ordinator of a core subject.

## Case study 12.3

E. is the music co-ordinator of a large primary school. The school has been described by Ofsted as being in a 'semi-rural and moderately disadvantaged area'. E. has been teaching for three years and his skills in music contributed towards his appointment. He had studied A-level music and played piano and recorder. During his teacher training course he played the piano for assemblies in a local school whenever possible.

E. became music co-ordinator from the outset. His role has included writing the school policy for music, which introduced a new published scheme that he felt would support members of staff less confident in the teaching of music. He has delivered in-service training for staff, and short- and medium-term targets have been set for the teaching of music. These include increasing staff interest, confidence and enthusiasm. E. is aware of what is going on in the school in terms of music teaching and has an overview to ensure progression, but he has not carried out any formal monitoring.

He has audited and ordered new resources and organised peripatetic music teachers to teach various instruments to the children. He and another teacher teach recorder. It is in the area of extra-curricular music that E. really comes into his own, and his title of 'Director of Performing Arts' says it all. He started with a small choir that involved Year 5 and Year 6 children. Now all Key Stage 2 year groups are represented, and some from Year 2. There are Christmas and summer productions and also 'Pop Stars' and 'Stars in their Eyes' competitions, where he takes a lead but is supported by other members of staff. He has organised a county-wide music competition and has represented the LEA at a national discussion meeting on widening musical opportunities for children. He writes lyrics and composes music. He has recently had the sad task of writing music for a CD dedicated to a pupil in the school who was killed, along with his sister, in a car crash. The child's parents and other children in the school were very appreciative of this.

## Case study 12.4

L. is the English co-ordinator in the same primary school as E. She is also the deputy head teacher. L. has been teaching for about 30 years and has been English co-ordinator for most of those years. She has really seen the role grow and has written three or four English policies over the years to reflect new initiatives. Recently, she has been given a new challenge with the amalgamation of the infant and junior schools. From co-ordinating Key Stage 2 English she now has to oversee the teaching at Key Stage 1, although she is very appreciative of the support given to her by a Key Stage 1 colleague.

Along with every other English co-ordinator in the country, L. has attended all the National Literacy Strategy training and has disseminated the information to her colleagues, supporting them where she can. She monitors teaching throughout the school. This is perhaps more readily accepted by the staff because of her status as deputy head teacher, her many years of experience and the importance of English as a core subject. L. also keeps parents informed of developments in terms of English teaching in the school although her Key Stage 1 colleagues do more of this work.

The management of resources is very much part of L.'s remit, ordering books for home reading and guided reading activities being a never-ending job.

L. finds that much of her role relates to whole-school target setting and SAT results. All members of staff are involved in the analysis of results and target setting but she oversees the progress where the targets relate to the teaching of English.

There is still time to enhance the English curriculum in terms of book events but the emphasis is very much on SAT results and target setting.

How typical are these roles? You might like to compare them with research carried out by Wragg *et al.* (1998) into the role of the English co-ordinator. Interviewees were asked to give a description of their role (*ibid.*: 95–6) and then the researchers categorised the individual responsibilities in terms of the categories described in the Ofsted (1994) publication *Primary Matters*. In this publication Her Majesty's Inspectors set out the following responsibilities:

**(a)** to develop a clear view of the nature of their subject and its contribution to the wider curriculum of the school;

**(b)** to provide advice and documentation to help teachers to teach the subject and interrelate its constituent elements;

**(c)** to play a major part in organising the teaching and learning resources of the subject so that statutory requirements are covered.

(*ibid.*: 9)

Wragg *et al.* (1998) found that co-ordinators described exactly those activities outlined by Ofsted, but there were some additions. In the case of English these included organising bookshops and literacy events. Many responses also included enthusiasm for the subject. Our case studies certainly described co-ordinators who were enthusiastic about their subjects but whose roles were dependent upon whether their area of responsibility related to a core or foundation subject. As long as there are SATs and league tables the co-ordinators of maths, English and science are going to focus on their pupils' levels of attainment. How confident do you feel that you could carry out this responsibility, with support, in your second year of teaching?

Activities 12.5 and 12.6 and the case studies of subject co-ordinators should give you some idea of what is expected. Co-ordinating a subject is challenging and it is a role that has grown radically in recent years but it is also a very exciting role and one that can provide a lot of satisfaction.

## Activity 12.6

Which subject do you think you could confidently co-ordinate? Answer the following questions relating to that subject:

- Do you have the necessary subject knowledge?
- Are you aware of recent national initiatives?
- Are you aware of recent research evidence?
- Have you read the most recent publications from government and other national bodies?
- Do you know what national inspection evidence tells us about different aspects of teaching in your subject?
- Would you be able to draw up whole-school planning and curriculum guidance?
- Would you be able to set targets for the whole school?
- Would you have the confidence to monitor teaching to ensure that the teaching of your subject was effective?

## Conclusion

It has been the aim of this book to encourage you to reflect on all aspects of your teaching. As the Teacher Training Agency becomes the Teaching Development Agency, it is an opportune time for you to realise that this reflection should be maintained as your career in education develops. This is not always easy when new initiatives are coming at you 'thick and fast' but your teaching will always be more effective if you think carefully about the rationale behind suggested changes. The first chapter of this book welcomed you to a career that is both challenging and rewarding. I hope the book, with its advice from contributors who have taught for many years, has helped you on your way.

## Suggestions for further reading

Bleach, K. (2001) *The Induction and Mentoring of Newly Qualified Teachers: A New Deal for Teachers.* London: David Fulton.

This book, with the help of case studies, activities and readings, will take you through your first year of teaching, considering your development from novice teacher to reflective practitioner.

Bubb, S. (2004) *The Insider's Guide for New Teachers.* London: RoutledgeFalmer.

This includes very good advice on applying for jobs and making the most of your induction year. Meetings with mentors, action plans and observing others are just some of the topics addressed.

*The Times Educational Supplement*

This weekly journal is a useful source of information about teaching posts in England, Scotland and Wales.

# References

DfEE (1999) *The Induction Period for Newly Qualified Teachers* (Circular 5/99). London: DfEE.

Ofsted (1994) *Primary Matters: A Discussion on Teaching and Learning in Primary Schools*. London: Ofsted Publications.

TTA (2003) *Career Entry and Development Profile*. London: Teacher Training Agency.

Wragg, E., Wragg, C.M., Haynes, G.S. and Chamberlin, R.P. (1998) *Improving Literacy in the Primary School*. London: Routledge.

# Index